TABLE OF CONTENTS

Top 20 Test Taking Tips

1. Carefully follow all the test registration procedures
2. Know the test directions, duration, topics, question types, how many questions
3. Setup a flexible study schedule at least 3-4 weeks before test day
4. Study during the time of day you are most alert, relaxed, and stress free
5. Maximize your learning style; visual learner use visual study aids, auditory learner use auditory study aids
6. Focus on your weakest knowledge base
7. Find a study partner to review with and help clarify questions
8. Practice, practice, practice
9. Get a good night's sleep; don't try to cram the night before the test
10. Eat a well balanced meal
11. Know the exact physical location of the testing site; drive the route to the site prior to test day
12. Bring a set of ear plugs; the testing center could be noisy
13. Wear comfortable, loose fitting, layered clothing to the testing center; prepare for it to be either cold or hot during the test
14. Bring at least 2 current forms of ID to the testing center
15. Arrive to the test early; be prepared to wait and be patient
16. Eliminate the obviously wrong answer choices, then guess the first remaining choice
17. Pace yourself; don't rush, but keep working and move on if you get stuck
18. Maintain a positive attitude even if the test is going poorly
19. Keep your first answer unless you are positive it is wrong
20. Check your work, don't make a careless mistake

Reading and Literacy

Linguistics and grammar

Linguistics is the branch of knowledge that deals with language. It is concerned with the lexical and grammatical categories of individual languages, the differences between languages, and the historical relationships between families of languages. Each lexical entry informs us about the linguistic properties of the word. It indicates a word's phonological, grammatical, and somatic properties.

Grammar, an integral part of linguistics, in its widest sense includes the study of the structure of words and syntactic constructions, and that of sound systems. Grammar may be said to generate a set of phrases and sentences, so linguistics is also the study of generative grammar. Grammar must also contain a phonological component, since this determines the phonetic form of words in speech. Phonology, the study of sound systems and processes affecting the way words are pronounced, is another aspect of linguistics.

Neurolinguistics

Neurolinguistics is concerned with the physical representations of linguistic processes in the brain. The most effective way to study this is to observe the effects on language capacity in brain-injured individuals. The frontal lobe of the brain appears to be the area responsible for controlling the production of speech. As research has become more refined over the years, it is evident that language functions are located in different parts of the brain. As improved diagnostic and sophisticated imaging techniques are developed, it is anticipated that the mysteries of language capacity and competence corresponding to specific parts of the brain will become clearer. For now, our knowledge in this field is imperfect, and the process of mapping the brain for linguistic capacity and performance is limited. Neurolinguistics is closely tied to neurology and neuro-physiology.

Phonetics

Phonetics seeks to provide a descriptive terminology for the sounds of spoken language. This includes the physiology for the production of speech sounds, the classification of speech sounds including vowels and consonants, the dynamic features of speech production, and the study of instrumental phonetics, the investigation of human speech by laboratory techniques. The dynamic aspects of phonetics include voice quality, stress, rhythm, and speech melody.

Instrumental phonetics underlines both the complexity of speech production, and the subtlety of the human brain in interpreting a constantly changing flow of acoustic data as recognizable speech-sounds. The correlation between acoustic quality, auditory perception, and articulatory position is a complex and not yet fully understood process. It represents a fertile area of research for phoneticians, psychologists, and perhaps philosophers.

Nouns and pronouns

Nouns name persons, places, things, animals, objects, time, feelings, concepts, and actions, and are usually signaled by an article (a, an, the). Nouns sometimes function as adjectives modifying other nouns. Nouns used in this manner are called noun/adjectives. Nouns are classified for a number of purposes: capitalization, word choice, count/no count nouns, and collective nouns are examples.

A pronoun is a word <u>used in place of</u> a noun: he, it, them, her, me, and so on. Usually the pronoun substitutes for the specific noun, called the antecedent. Although most pronouns function as substitutes for nouns, some can function as adjectives modifying nouns. Pronouns may be classed as personal, possessive, intensive, relative, interrogative, demonstrative, indefinite, and reciprocal. Pronouns can cause a number of problems for writers, including pronoun-antecedent agreement, distinguishing between who and whom, and differentiating pronouns, such as I and me. Four frequently encountered problems with pronouns include the following:

- Pronoun-antecedent agreement: The antecedent of a pronoun is the word the pronoun refers to. A pronoun and its antecedent agree when they are both singular or plural, or of the same gender.
- Pronoun reference: A pronoun should refer clearly to its antecedent. A pronoun's reference will be unclear if it is ambiguous, implied, vague, or indefinite.
- Personal pronouns: Some pronouns change their case form according to their grammatical structure in a sentence. Pronouns functioning as subjects appear in the subjective case, those functioning as objects appear in the objective case, and those functioning as possessives appear in the possessive case.
- Who or whom: Who, a subjective-case pronoun, can be used only as subjects and subject complements. Whom, an objective-case pronoun, can be used only for objects. The words who and whom appear primarily in subordinate clauses or in questions.

Verbs

The verb of a sentence usually expresses action or being. It is composed of a main verb and sometimes supporting verbs. These helping verbs are forms of have, do, and be, and nine modals. The modals are can, could, may, might, shall, should, will, would, and ought. Some verbs are followed by words that look like prepositions but are so closely associated with the verb that they are part of its meaning. These words are known as particles, and examples include call off, look up, and drop off. The main verb of a sentence is always one that would change form from base form to past tense, past participle, present participle, and –s forms. When both the past-tense and past-participle forms of a verb end in –ed, the verb is regular. In all other cases, the verb is irregular. The verb to be is highly irregular, having eight forms instead of the usual five.

Linking verbs, transitive verbs, and intransitive verbs
Linking verbs link the subject to a subject complement, a word, or word group that completes the meaning of the subject by renaming or describing it.
A transitive verb takes a direct object, a word, or word group that names a receiver of the action. The direct object of a transitive verb is sometimes preceded by an indirect object. Transitive verbs usually appear in the active voice, with a subject doing the action and a direct object receiving the action. The direct object of a transitive verb is sometimes followed by an object complement, a word or word group that completes the direct object's meaning by renaming or describing it. Intransitive verbs take no objects or complements. Their pattern is subject + verb.
A dictionary will disclose whether a verb is transitive or intransitive. Some verbs have both transitive and intransitive functions.

Subject/verb agreement
In the present tense, verbs agree with their subjects in number, (singular or plural) and in person (first, second, or third). The present tense ending –s is used with a verb if its subject is third person singular; otherwise, the verb takes no ending. The verb to be varies from this pattern, and, alone among verbs, it has special forms in both the present and past tense.

Problems with subject-verb agreement tend to arise in certain contexts:
- Words between subject and verbs
- Subjects joined by and
- Subjects joined by or or nor
- Indefinite pronouns, such as someone
- Collective nouns
- Subject after the verb
- Pronouns who, which, and that
- Plural form, singular meaning
- Titles, company names, and words mentioned as words

Verbal phrases
A verbal phrase is a verb form that does not function as the verb of a clause. There are three major types of verbal phrases:
- Participial phrases: These always function as adjectives. Their verbals are always present participles, always ending in –ing, or past participles frequently ending in –d,–ed,–n,–en, or –t. Participial phrases frequently appear immediately following the noun or pronoun they modify.
- Gerund phrases: Gerund phrases are built around present participles, and they always function as nouns, usually as subjects, subject complements, direct objects, or objects of a preposition.
- Infinitive phrases are usually structured around to plus the base form of the verb. They can function as nouns, as adjectives, or as adverbs. When functioning as a noun, an infinitive phrase may appear in almost any noun slot in a sentence, usually as a subject, subject complement, or direct object. Infinitive phrases functioning as adjectives usually appear immediately following the noun or pronoun they modify. Adverbial phrases usually qualify the meaning of the verb.

Problems with verbs
The verb is the heart of the sentence. Verbs have several potential problems, including the following:
- Irregular verbs: These are verbs that do not follow usual grammatical rules.
- Tense: Tenses indicate the time of an action in relation to the time of speaking or writing about the action.
- Mood: There are three moods in English: the indicative, used for facts, opinions, and questions; the imperative, used for orders or advice; and the subjunctive, used for wishes. The subjunctive mood is the most likely to cause problems. The subjunctive mood is used for wishes and in if clauses expressing conditions contrary to facts. The subjunctive, in such cases, is the past tense form of the verb; in the case of be, it is always were, even if the subject is singular. The subjunctive mood is also used in that clauses following verbs such as ask, insist, recommend, and request. The subjunctive, in such cases, is the base, or dictionary, form of the verb.

Adjectives, adverbs, and articles

Adjectives modify nouns or pronouns; adverbs modify verbs, adjectives, or other adverbs. An adjective is a word used to modify or describe a noun or pronoun. An adjective usually answers one of these questions: Which one? What kind? How many? Adjectives usually precede the words they modify although they sometimes follow linking verbs, in which case they describe the subject.

When an adjective functions as a subject complement, it describes the subject. Adjectives are often misused in place of adverbs to modify verbs in casual or nonstandard speech. An adverb is a word used to modify or qualify a verb, adjective, or another adverb. It usually answers one of these questions: When? Where? How? Why? Adverbs modifying adjectives or other adverbs usually intensify or limit the intensity of words they modify. Many adverbs are formed by adding –ly to adjectives. However, not all words ending in –ly are adverbs. Some adjectives end in –ly, and some adverbs do not. The negators not and never are classified as adverbs. Writers sometimes misuse adverbs, and multilingual speakers have trouble placing them correctly. Most adjectives and adverbs have three forms: the positive, the comparative, and the superlative. The comparative should be used to compare two things, the superlative to compare three or more things. Articles, sometimes classed as adjectives, are used to mark nouns. There are only three: the definite article the and the indefinite articles a and an.

Classification of sentences

Sentences are classified in two ways: according to their structure or to their purpose. Writers use declarative sentences to make statements, imperative sentences to issue requests or commands, interrogative sentences to ask questions, and exclamatory sentences to make exclamations. Depending on the number and types of clauses they contain, sentences may be classified as simple, compound, complex, or compound-complex.

Clauses come in two varieties: independent and subordinate. An independent clause is a full sentence pattern that does not function within another sentence pattern; it contains a subject and modifiers plus a verb and any objects, complements, and modifiers of that verb, and it either stands alone or could stand alone. A subordinate clause is a full sentence pattern that functions within a sentence as an adjective, an adverb, or a noun but cannot stand alone as a complete sentence.

Sentence structure

The four major types of sentence structure are:
- Simple sentences: Simple sentences have one independent clause with no subordinate clauses. A simple sentence may contain compound elements—a compound subject, verb, or object, for example—but does not contain more than one full sentence pattern.
- Compound sentences: Compound sentences are composed of two or more independent clauses with no subordinate clauses. The independent clauses are usually joined with a comma and a coordinating conjunction or with a semicolon.
- Complex sentences: A complex sentence is composed of one independent clause with one or more dependent clauses.
- Compound-complex sentences: A compound-complex sentence contains at least two independent clauses and at least one subordinate clause. Sometimes they contain two full sentence patterns that can stand alone. When each independent clause contains a subordinate clause, this makes the sentence both compound and complex.

Subject of a sentence

The subject of a sentence names who or what the sentence is about. The complete subject is composed of the simple subject and all of its modifiers. To find the complete subject, ask, who? Or, what? Insert the verb to complete the question. The answer is the complete subject. To find the simple subject, strip away all the modifiers in the complete subject.

In imperative sentences, the verb's subject is understood, but not actually present in the sentence. Although the subject ordinarily comes before the verb, in sentences that begin with There are or

There was, the subject follows the verb. The ability to recognize the subject of a sentence helps in editing a variety of problems, such as sentence fragments and subject-verb agreement, as well as the choice of pronouns.

Prepositions and conjunctions

A preposition is a word placed before a noun or pronoun to form a phrase modifying another word in the sentence. The prepositional phrase usually functions as an adjective or adverb. There are a limited number of prepositions in English, perhaps around 80. Some prepositions are more than one word long. Along with, listen to, and next to are some examples. Conjunctions join words, phrases, or clauses, and they indicate the relationship between the elements that are joined. There are coordinating conjunctions that connect grammatically equal elements, correlative conjunctions that connect pairs, subordinating conjunctions that introduce a subordinate clause, and conjunctive adverbs, which may be used with a semicolon to connect independent clauses. The most common conjunctive adverbs include then, thus, and however. Using conjunctions correctly helps avoid sentence fragments and run-on sentences.

Modes of sentence patterns

Sentence patterns fall into five common modes with some exceptions. They are:
1. Subject + linking verb + subject complement
2. Subject + transitive verb + direct object
3. Subject + transitive verb + indirect object + direct object
4. Subject + transitive verb + direct object + object complement
5. Subject + intransitive verb

Common exceptions to these patterns are questions and commands, sentences with delayed subjects, and passive transformations. Writers sometimes use the passive voice when the active voice would be more appropriate.

Subordinate word groups

Subordinate word groups cannot stand alone. They function only within sentences, as adjectives, adverbs, or nouns.
Prepositional phrases begin with a preposition and end with a noun or noun equivalent, called its object. Prepositional phrases function as adjectives or adverbs.
Subordinate clauses are patterned like sentences, having subjects, verbs, and objects or complements. They function within sentences as adverbs, adjectives, or nouns.
Adjective clauses modify nouns or pronouns and begin with a relative pronoun or relative adverb.
Adverb clauses modify verbs, adjectives, and other adverbs.
Noun clauses function as subjects, objects, or complements. In both adjective and noun clauses words may appear out of their normal order. The parts of a noun clause may also appear in their normal order.

Appositive and absolute phrases

Strictly speaking, appositive phrases are not subordinate word groups. Appositive phrases function somewhat as adjectives do, to describe nouns or pronouns. Instead of modifying nouns or pronouns, however, appositive phrases rename them. In form, they are nouns or noun equivalents. Appositives are said to be in apposition to the nouns or pronouns they rename. For example, in the sentence "Terriers, hunters at heart, have been dandied up to look like lap dogs," hunters at heart is in apposition to the noun terriers.

An absolute phrase modifies a whole clause or sentence, not just one word, and it may appear nearly anywhere in the sentence. It consists of a noun or noun equivalent usually followed by a participial phrase. Both appositive and absolute phrases can cause confusion in their usage in grammatical structures. They are particularly difficult for a person whose first language is not English.

Sentence fragments

As a rule, a part of a sentence should not be treated as a complete sentence. A sentence must be composed of at least one full independent clause. An independent clause has a subject and a verb and can stand alone as a sentence. Some fragments are clauses that contain a subject and a verb but begin with a subordinating word. Other fragments lack a subject, verb, or both. A sentence fragment can be repaired by combining the fragment with a nearby sentence, punctuating the new sentence correctly, or turning the fragment into a sentence by adding the missing elements. Some sentence fragments are used by writers for emphasis. Although sentence fragments are sometimes acceptable, readers and writers do not always agree on when they are appropriate. A conservative approach is to write in complete sentences only unless a special circumstance dictates otherwise.

Run-on sentences

Run-on sentences are independent clauses that have not been joined correctly. An independent clause is a word group that does or could stand alone in a sentence. When two or more independent clauses appear in one sentence, they must be joined in one of these ways:
- Revision with a comma and a coordinating conjunction
- Revision with a semicolon, a colon, or a dash, used when independent clauses are closely related and their relationship is clear without a coordinating conjunction
- Revision by separating sentences, used when both independent clauses are long or if one is a question and one is not: Separate sentences may be the best option in this case.
- Revision by restructuring the sentence: For sentence variety, consider restructuring the sentence, perhaps by turning one of the independent clauses into a subordinate phrase or clause.

Usually one of these choices will be an obvious solution to the run-on sentence. The fourth technique above is often the most effective solution but requires the most revision.

Examining paragraphs and sentences

Paragraphs are a key structural unit of prose used to break up long stretches of words into more manageable subsets and to indicate a shift in topics or focus. Each paragraph may be examined by identifying the main point of the section and ensuring that every sentence supports or relates to the main theme. Paragraphs may be checked to make sure the organization used in each is appropriate and that the number of sentences is adequate to develop the topic. Sentences are the building blocks of the written word, and they can be varied by paying attention to sentence length, sentence structure, and sentence openings. These elements should be varied so that writing does not seem boring, repetitive, or choppy. A careful analysis of a piece of writing will expose these stylistic problems, and they can be corrected before the final draft is written. Varying sentence structure and length can make writing more inviting and appealing to a reader.

Revising and editing sentences

Revising sentences is done to make writing more effective. Editing sentences is done to correct any errors. Revising sentences is usually best done on a computer, on which it is possible to try several versions easily. Some writers prefer to print out a hard copy and work with this for revisions. Each works equally well and depends on the individual preference.

Spelling and grammar checks on software are a great aid to a writer, but not a panacea. Many grammatical problems—such as faulty parallelism, mixed constructions, and misplaced modifiers—can slip past the programs. Even if errors are caught, the writing still must be evaluated for effectiveness. A combination of software programs and writer awareness is necessary to ensure an error-free manuscript.

Main point of a paragraph

A paragraph should be unified around a main point. A good topic sentence summarizes the paragraph's main point. A topic sentence is more general than subsequent supporting sentences are. Sometime the topic sentence will be used to close the paragraph if earlier sentences give a clear indication of the direction of the paragraph. Sticking to the main point means deleting or omitting unnecessary sentences that do not advance the main point.

The main point of a paragraph deserves adequate development, which usually means a substantial paragraph. A paragraph of two or three sentences often does not develop a point well enough, particularly if the point is a strong supporting argument of the thesis. An occasional short paragraph is fine, particularly if it is used as a transitional device. A choppy appearance should be avoided.

Double negatives and double superlatives

Standard English allows two negatives only if a positive meaning is intended. "The team was not displeased with its performance" is an example. Double negatives used to emphasize negation are nonstandard.

Negative modifiers—such as never, no, and not—should not be paired with other negative modifiers or negative words, such as none, nobody, nothing, and neither. The modifiers hardly, barely, and scarcely are also considered negatives in Standard English, so they should not be used with other negatives, such as not, no one, or never.

Do not use double superlatives or comparatives. When –er or –est has been added to an adjective or adverb, avoid using more or most. Avoid expressions such as more perfect and very round. Either something is or is not. It is not logical to suggest that absolute concepts come in degrees. Use the comparative to compare two things and the superlative to compare three or more things.

Commas

The comma was invented to help readers. Without it, sentence parts can run together, making meanings unclear. Various rules for comma use include the following:
- Use a comma between a coordinating conjunction joining independent clauses.
- Use a comma after an introductory clause or phrase.
- Use a comma between items in a series.
- Use a comma between coordinate adjectives not joined with and. Do not use a comma between cumulative adjectives.
- Use commas to set off nonrestrictive elements. Do not use commas to set off restrictive elements.

- Use commas to set off transitional and parenthetical expressions, absolute phrases, and elements expressing contrast.
- Use commas to set off nouns of direct address, the words yes and no, interrogative tags, and interjections.
- Use commas with dates, addresses, titles, and numbers.
- Use commas to prevent confusion.
- Use commas to set off direct quotations.

The following are some situations in which commas are unnecessary:
- Do not use a comma between compound elements that are not independent clauses.
- Do not use a comma after a phrase that begins with an inverted sentence.
- Do not use a comma between the first or after the last item in a series or before the word although.
- Do not use a comma between cumulative adjectives, between an adjective and a noun, or between an adverb and an adjective.
- Do not use commas to set off restrictive or mildly parenthetical elements or to set off an indirect quotation.
- Do not use a comma to set off a concluding adverb clause that is essential to the meaning of the sentence or after the word although.
- Do not use a comma to separate a verb from its subject or object. 8. Do not use a comma after a coordinating conjunction or before a parenthesis.
- Do not use a comma with a question mark or an exclamation point.

Semicolons

The semicolon is used to connect major sentence elements of equal grammatical rank. Some rules regarding semicolons include the following:
- Use a semicolon between closely related independent clauses not joined with a coordinating conjunction.
- Use a semicolon between independent clauses linked with a transitional expression.
- Use a semicolon between items in a series containing internal punctuation.
- Avoid using a semicolon between a subordinate clause and the rest of the sentence.
- Avoid using a semicolon between an appositive word and the word it refers to.
- Avoid using a semicolon to introduce a list.
- Avoid using a semicolon between independent clauses joined by and, but, or, nor, for, so, or yet.

Colons

The colon is used primarily to call attention to the words that follow it. In addition, the colon has some other conventional uses:
- Use a colon after an independent clause to direct attention to a list, an appositive, or a quotation.
- Use a colon between independent clauses if the second summarizes or explains the first.
- Use a colon after the salutation in a formal letter, to indicate hours and minutes, to show proportions, between a title and subtitle, and between city and publisher in bibliographic entries.

A colon must be preceded by a full independent clause. Avoid using colons in the following situations:
- Between a verb and its object or complement
- Between a preposition and its object
- After such as, including, or for example

Apostrophe

An apostrophe is used to indicate that a noun is possessive. Possessive nouns usually indicate ownership, as in Bill's coat or the dog's biscuit. Sometimes ownership is only loosely implied, as in the dog's coat or the forest's trees. If it is unclear whether a noun is possessive, turning into phrase may clarify it.

If the noun is plural and ends in–s, add only an apostrophe. To show joint possession, use –'s with the last noun only. To show individual possession, make all nouns possessive.

An apostrophe is often optional in plural numbers, letters, abbreviations, and words mentioned as words. Common errors in using apostrophes include the following:
- Using an apostrophe with nouns that are not possessive
- Using an apostrophe in the possessive pronouns its, whose, his, hers, ours, yours, and theirs

Dashes, parentheses, and brackets

Dashes are used for the following purposes:
- To set off parenthetical material that deserves emphasis
- To set off appositives that contain commas
- To prepare for a list, a restatement, an amplification, or a dramatic shift in tone or thought

Unless there is a specific reason for using the dash, omit it. It can give text a choppy effect. Parentheses are used to enclose supplemental material, minor digressions, and afterthoughts. They are also used to enclose letters or numbers, labeling them items in a series. Parentheses should be used sparingly, as they break up text in a distracting manner when overused. Brackets are used to enclose any words or phrases that have been inserted into an otherwise word-for-word quotation.

End punctuations

Use a period to end all sentences except direct questions or genuine exclamations. Periods should be used in abbreviations according to convention. Problems can arise when there is a choice between a period and a question mark or exclamation point. If a sentence reports a question rather than asking it directly, it should end with a period, not a question mark.

Question marks should be used following a direct question. If a polite request is written in the form of a question, it may be followed by a period. Questions in a series may be followed by question marks even when they are not in complete sentences. Exclamation marks are used after a word group or sentence that expresses exceptional feeling or deserves special emphasis. Exclamation marks should not be overused, being reserved for appropriate exclamatory interjections.

Quotation marks

The uses of quotation marks are as follows:
- Use quotation marks to enclose direct quotations of a person's words, spoken or written. Do not use quotation marks around indirect quotations. An indirect quotation reports someone's ideas without using that person's exact words.

- Set off long quotations of prose or poetry by indenting.
- Use single quotation marks to enclose a quotation within a quotation.
- Quotation marks should be used around the titles of short works: newspaper and magazine articles, poems, short stories, songs, episodes of television and radio programs, and subdivisions of books or web sites.
- Punctuation is used with quotation marks according to convention. Periods and commas are placed inside quotation marks, whereas colons and semicolons are placed outside quotation marks. Question marks and exclamation points are placed either inside or outside quotation marks, depending on the rest of the material in the sentence.
- Do not use quotation marks around the title of your own essay.

Ellipsis marks and slashes

The ellipsis mark consists of three spaced periods (...) and is used to indicate when certain words have been deleted from an otherwise word-for-word quotation. If a full sentence or more is deleted in the middle of a quoted passage, a period should be inserted before the ellipsis dots. The ellipsis mark should not be used at the beginning of a quotation. It should also not be used at the end of a quotation unless some words have been deleted from the end of the final sentence.
The slash (/) may be used to separate two or three lines of poetry that have been run into a text. If there are more than three lines of poetry they should be handled as an indented quotation. The slash may occasionally be used to separate paired terms such as passed/failed or either/or. In this case, a space is not placed before or after the slash. The slash should be used sparingly, only when it is clearly appropriate.

Analogies and cause and effect

Analogies draw comparisons between items that appear to have nothing in common. Analogies are employed by writers to attempt to provoke fresh thoughts and changed feelings about a subject. They may be used to make the unfamiliar more familiar, to clarify an abstract point, or to argue a point. Although analogies are effective literary devices, they should be used thoughtfully in arguments. Two things may be alike in some respects but completely different in others.

Cause and effect is an excellent device best used when the cause and effect are generally accepted as true. As a matter of argument, cause and effect is usually too complex and subject to other interpretations to be used successfully. A valid way of using cause and effect is to state the effect in the topic sentence of a paragraph and add the causes in the body of the paragraph. This adds logic and form to a paragraph and usually makes it more effective.

Point of view

Point of view is the perspective from which writing occurs. There are several possibilities:
- First person is written so that the I of the story is a participant or observer.
- Second person is a device to draw the reader in more closely. It is really a variation or refinement of the first-person narrative.
- Third person, the most traditional form of point of view, is the omniscient narrator, in which the narrative voice, presumed to be the writer's, is presumed to know everything about the characters, plot, and action. Most novels use this point of view.
- A multiple point of view is narration delivered from the perspective of several characters.

In modern writing, the stream-of-consciousness technique is often used. Developed fully by James Joyce, this technique uses an interior monologue that provides the narration through the thoughts, impressions, and fantasies of the narrator.

Analogy, simile, and metaphors

An analogy is a literary device that compares two things. It functions as an extended metaphor. In a broader sense, analogies refer to the process of reasoning from parallel examples. Similes are figures of speech that use a grammatical connection, such as like, as if, or as to explain comparisons. Metaphors, in a narrow sense, are figures of speech that highlight the similarities between two elements, conventionally called tenor and vehicle. Metaphors may be direct or indirect. A direct metaphor states the comparison directly, whereas an indirect metaphor only implies the comparison. Metaphors have always been a major device in poetry and are now seen in every aspect of language. All these literary devices are used to enrich and emphasize observed qualities. They are present in all genres.

Hyperbole, personification, and foreshadowing

Hyperbole is a figure of speech that uses extreme exaggeration for dramatic effect. It usually functions to compare and is used quite often in romantic works. Love poetry is an example of a subgenre that fosters the use of hyperbole. Hyperbole may also be used farcically for comic effect. Personification is another figure of speech, which attributes human qualities to an inanimate object or abstract entity. Personification helps us to use our self-knowledge and extrapolate it to understand abstract concepts, forces of nature, and common events. Personification is sometimes achieved by similes or analogies to strengthen the imagery. Foreshadowing uses hints in a narrative to let the audience anticipate future events in the plot. Foreshadowing can be indicated by a number of literary devices and figures of speech, as well as through dialogue between characters. In Ibsen's play Hedda Gabler, Hedda plays with a gun early in the play, which foreshadows her eventual suicide. In Shakespeare's Macbeth, the three witches in the opening scene foreshadow horrific events to come. Examples abound in all forms of literature but are perhaps most evident in drama.

Protagonists, antagonists, heroes, and villains

A protagonist is the central character in a play or story. The character opposing the protagonist is called the antagonist. Either may be the hero or villain of a drama or work of fiction. In modern literature, the protagonist–antagonist struggle is often represented as an internal conflict in one individual. Freudian thought has had a great influence on this inward battle of psychological forces in a person. The hero or heroine is also the major figure in a literary work. The term may be used instead of protagonist. Finally, the villain is the major evil character in a literary work. Usually the villain opposes the protagonist but sometimes is the protagonist of a work. The roles of heroes and villains are exaggerated in melodrama and often seen in early films. The conflict in these cases usually involves a fair damsel. Modern literature usually reflects a more mixed character, with both qualities present in a character.

Climax, anticlimax, and closure

A climax occurs when a state of tension in a literary work reaches its peak, usually with a resolution of some kind. There may be many or only one climax in a work, depending on the plotting and length of the story. A climax is usually preceded by an increasing level of tension, usually between the protagonist and antagonist. The climax may take the form of action, speech, or symbolism. An anticlimax occurs in fiction or drama when a critical point in the work is resolved and the dramatic tension recedes. The term can be used negatively if it refers to a weakness in a drama or story. Sometimes an anticlimax is used to enhance a scene or serve as a respite from a period of action. Closure is the modification of the structure of a work that makes absence of further development unlikely. It creates the expectation of nothing and leaves the reader or audience satisfied that the plot development is over. Closure often has a dramatic force of its own and sometimes is the final climax.

Purposes of writing and audience analysis

Discovering a purpose is an important first step in writing. Here are some common purposes for writing:
To inform, persuade, change attitudes, to analyze, argue, theorize, summarize, evaluate, recommend, to request, propose, provoke, to express feelings, to entertain, and to give pleasure are all legitimate purposes in writing.
It is a common error to misjudge the purpose of a writing assignment. A writer would do well to ask "Why am I communicating with my readers?", before undertaking a specific assignment. Another important question that follows is "Just who are those readers?" Audience analysis can sometimes suggest an effective strategy for reaching the readers. Sometimes audiences do not fall into a neat category, but are mixed in interest and purpose. This presents additional challenges to the writer.

Literary genres

Literary genres refer to the basic generic types of poetry, drama, fiction, and nonfiction. Literary genre is a method of classifying and analyzing literature. There are numerous subdivisions within genre, including such categories as novels, novellas, and short stories in fiction. Drama may also be subdivided into comedy, tragedy, and many other categories. Poetry and nonfiction have their own distinct divisions.
Genres often overlap, and the distinctions among them are blurred, such as that between the nonfiction novel and docudrama, as well as many others. However, the use of genres is helpful to the reader as a set of understandings that guide our responses to a work. The generic norm sets expectations and forms the framework within which we read and evaluate a work. This framework will guide both our understanding and interpretation of the work. It is a useful tool for both literary criticism and analysis.

Fiction

Fiction is a general term for any form of literary narrative that is invented or imagined rather than being factual. For those individuals who equate fact with truth, the imagined or invented character of fiction tends to render it relatively unimportant or trivial among the genres. Defenders of fiction are quick to point out that the fictional mode is an essential part of being. The ability to imagine or discuss what-if plots, characters, and events is clearly part of the human experience.
Fiction is much wider than simply prose fiction. Songs, ballads, epics, and narrative poems are examples of non-prose fiction. A full definition of fiction must include not only the work itself but also the framework in which it is read. Literary fiction can also be defined as not true rather than nonexistent, as many works of historical fiction refer to real people, places, and events that are treated imaginatively as if they were true. These imaginary elements enrich and broaden literary expression.

Poetry

Reading poetry
Some general guidelines for reading poetry may be summarized as follows:
- Understand the relationship of the title to the work. Does the title suggest anything about the subject?
- Ascertain who the "speaker" of the poem is. Determine what type of narrative is employed.
- Know the major theme or argument that dominates the work.
- Poems deal with private or individual matters or subjects in the public spectrum. Determine which the poem is addressing.
- What type of meter is used in the poem? Is rhyme employed as a device?
- Carefully examine the poem for figurative language and note how it is used.
- Be aware of the poems historical and cultural setting to place the meaning in context.
- Notice whether the poem fits a formally defined genre within poetry.

Figurative language
Poetry is a genre in which language is used in all its variations and embellishments to convey a sense, mood, or feeling the poet deems important. Poetry uses elaborate linguistic constructions to explain the world in creative ways. Poetry manipulates language itself to convey impressions in new and innovative constructions. It makes extensive use of figurative devices—such as conceits, similes, metaphors, and many more—to express things in fresh ways. Poets use figurative language to suggest rather than give direct meanings. This language provides a creative experience for the reader, who is asked to understand meaning in unconventional terms. Poets relish opportunities to express themselves in creative and unusual words. Figurative language provides both poet and reader an opportunity for unique expression and understanding. Emotions, feelings, and moods are evoked by the skillful use of figurative language.

Drama

Drama is any work in which actors or actresses assume roles before an audience in a theatre, motion pictures, television, or radio. Drama is a major literary genre that may be subdivided into three major groups:
- Tragedy: a drama in which the leading character has a disastrous end. The character usually represents something significant, whether good or bad. Tragedy may be seen as an attempt to extract a value from human mortality, giving the subgenre a positive view of human life, despite its inevitable end.
- Tragicomedy: a drama that includes both comic and tragic elements. Tragicomedy thus results in a bittersweet mix of literary value. As George Bernard Shaw once commented, tragicomedy is a much deeper and grimmer entertainment than tragedy.
- Comedy: a type of drama that satirizes the misadventures of its characters. Comedy often emphasizes society and its mores rather than the individual (more common in tragedies). Its origins may be traced to the primitive celebrations of spring.

Prose

Prose is derived from the Latin and means "straightforward discourse." Prose fiction, although having many categories, may be divided into three main groups:

- Short stories: a fictional narrative, the length of which varies, usually under 20,000 words. Short stories usually have only a few characters and generally describe one major event or insight. The short story began in magazines in the late 1800s and has flourished ever since.
- Novels: a longer work of fiction, often containing a large cast of characters and extensive plotting. The emphasis may be on an event, action, social problems, or any experience. There is now a genre of nonfiction novels pioneered by Truman Capote's In Cold Blood in the 1960s. Novels may also be written in verse.
- Novellas: a work of narrative fiction longer than a short story but shorter than a novel. Novellas may also be called short novels or novelettes. They originated from the German tradition and have become common forms in all of the world's literature.

Narrative technique and tone

The following are important questions to address to better understand the voice and role of the narrator and incorporate that voice into an overall understanding of the novel:
- Who is the narrator of the novel? What is the narrator's perspective, first person or third person? What is the role of the narrator in the plot? Are there changes in narrators or the perspective of narrators?
- Does the narrator explain things in the novel, or does meaning emerge from the plot and events? The personality of the narrator is important. She may have a vested interest in a character or event described. Some narratives follow the time sequence of the plot, whereas others do not. A narrator may express approval or disapproval about a character or events in the work.
- Tone is an important aspect of the narration. Who is actually being addressed by the narrator? Is the tone familiar or formal, intimate or impersonal? Does the vocabulary suggest clues about the narrator?

Elegy

An elegy is a mournful or sorrowful poem, usually lamenting the dead. It typically expresses the poet's sorrow for the loss of a friend or lover, or more generally for the sadness of the human condition. Consolation is a recurring theme in an elegy, in some way consoling the audience for the brevity of human existence. The first elegy was "The Idylls of Theocritus," in early Greek literature. More modern examples include Milton's "Lycidas," Thomas Gray's "Elegy Written in a Country Church Yard," Shelley's "Adonais," and W. H. Auden's "In Memory of W. B. Yeats." In formal poetic convention, an elegy refers to any poem, regardless of subject, written in elegiac distiches (alternating lines of dactylic hexameter and pentameter). The usual understanding of the term in poetry is the sorrowful or mournful mood that is the signature of the elegy. This type of work is much less common in modern poetry although it still occurs.

Epic

Originally, epics were long narrative poems that focused on a hero's adventures and triumphs. The hero generally undergoes a series of trials that test his courage, character, and intellect. Epic poems have certain conventions, such as the use of a muse and exhaustive lists of armies, ships, and catalogues. These written and oral epics transmitted folk culture from generation to generation. The best known of the original epics were written by Homer and Virgil. Milton's "Paradise Lost" is an example of a more recent epic as is Cervantes's Don Quixote. Epic theatre, pioneered by Bertolt Brecht, is a further refinement of the form. Epics have come to mean any dramatic work of poetry, prose, drama, film, or music that depends on spectacles and lavish productions sometimes based on historical events.

Essays

Essays are usually defined as prose compositions dealing with one or two topics and are relatively brief (rarely exceeding 25 pages). The word essay is from the French essayer, meaning to try or attempt. The term was coined by Michel de Montaigne (1533–92), who is still regarded as a master of the form. Essays tend to be informal in style and are usually personal in approach and opinion. Francis Bacon (1561–1626) pioneered essays that were dogmatic and impersonal, leading to a division of essays called formal and familiar, respectively. The formal essays have dominated the professional and scientific fields, whereas the informal style is written primarily to entertain or give opinions.

Writers should be mindful of the style of essay their subject lends itself to and conform to the conventions of that style. Some types of essays, particularly scientific and academic writing, have style manuals to guide the format and conventions of the writing. The Modern Language Association and the American Psychological Association have two of the most widely followed style manuals. They are widely available for writers' reference. Some essays have been adapted to verse, whereas others are a hybrid of essay and fiction. Essays usually begin with an observation or musing on a subject. Formal essays tend to present an argument, whereas familiar essays are less dogmatic and reflect the personal views of the author. They do not try to convince but proffer opinions and observations on a subject. Essays have been written about countless subjects, from public policy to existential anxiety. Literary essays are popular, and some of the best were written by notable authors, such as Henry James, Virginia Woolf, and T. S. Eliot.

Thesis
A thesis states the main idea of the essay. A working or tentative thesis should be established early on in the writing process. This working thesis is subject to change and modification as writing progresses. It will serve to keep the writer focused as ideas develop.
The working thesis has two parts: a topic and a comment. The comment makes an important point about the topic. A working thesis should be interesting to an anticipated audience; it should be specific and limit the topic to a manageable scope. Three criteria are useful tools to measure the effectiveness of any working thesis. The writer applies these tools to ascertain the following:
- Is the topic of sufficient interest to hold an audience?
- Is the topic specific enough to generate interest?
- Is the topic manageable? Too broad? Too narrow? Can it be adequately researched?

Title, introduction, and conclusion
A good title can identify the subject, describe it in a colorful manner, and give clues to the approach and sometimes the conclusion of the writing. It usually defines the work in the mind of the reader. A strong introduction follows the lead of the title; it draws the readers into the work and clearly states the topic with a clarifying comment. A common style is to state the topic, and then provide additional details, finally leading to a statement of the thesis at the end. An introduction can also begin with an arresting quote, question, or strong opinion, which grabs the reader's attention.
A good conclusion should leave readers satisfied and provide a sense of closure. Many conclusions restate the thesis and formulate general statements that grow out of it. Writers often find ways to conclude in a dramatic fashion through a vivid image, quotation, or a warning. This in an effort to give the ending the punch to tie up any existing points.

Problem plays

Problem plays focus on social problems and movements. Alexander Dumas, son of the great French novelist, wrote a series of short plays attacking the ills of society. The early 19th century was the heyday of problem plays. Henrik Ibsen is perhaps the most celebrated of the problem plays playwright, particularly with his treatment of women's rights in "The Doll House". Lillian Hellman and Arthur Miller have both written popular problem plays in the 20th century.

The term, problem plays, is used in a different context by Shakespearean scholars. These critics use the term for plays that have caused interpretation problems for audiences. Plays such as "All's Well That Ends Well", "Troilus and Cressida", and "Measure for Measure" lend themselves to various interpretations and pose literary problems for students of the bard.

Ballads

The original meaning of ballad was song closely associated with dance. Over time, the ballad formed a branch of narrative using verse. Folk ballads, the most common form, typically deal with love affairs, tragic endings, and occasionally historical and military subjects. The narration is often told in dialogue form, arranged in quatrains with the second and fourth lines rhyming. Ballads are derived from folk tales and oral traditions and use direct, descriptive language. Ballads have been popular for centuries, and folk music is an extension of the ballad form. The term ballad is still used extensively to note songs that tell a story, usually with a romantic or tragic theme. Ballads are sometimes derived from historical sources, lending them a sense of stories told in verse. Minstrels were the early performers of ballads and were important in preserving the cultural and historical records of many peoples. Ballads have also been adopted by poets, as in Wilde's "The Ballad of Reading Gaol."

Progression of a dramatic plot

When studying dramatic works, significant events in the story should be recognized. Major shifts or reversals in the plot, and subsequent action should be followed carefully. Aristotle's "Poetics" described a typical progression pattern of a plot as follows:
1. Exposition
2. Complication
3. Reversal
4. Recognition
5. Resolution

This progression is still valid today as we study and analyze plots. The plot may follow the pattern of comedy (ending with a celebration), or tragedy (ending with death). The plot may be explained through dialogue, stage action, and off-stage events or by a chorus. While plots of well known plays are easily understood and analyzed, more esoteric drama requires more careful attention to the plot's complexities.

Children's literature

Children's literature is designed to be read and enjoyed primarily by young readers. Early children's literature was written exclusively for educational purposes. Beginning in the middle of the 18th century, children's books were written to entertain as well as edify. Adventure stories for boys became popular in the 19th century, as did fiction designed for girls, such as Louisa May Alcott's Little Women (1868) and Johanna Spyri's Heidi (1880). Mark Twain and Robert Louis Stevenson became important writers of children's fiction during this time. Recent years have emphasized more realism in children's literature. Opposed to the traditional view of shielding children from the realities of life, many now advocate books that are not only realistic but also tragic, providing an opportunity for catharsis for young readers. An example of this type of fiction is William Armstrong's Sounder (1969), a novel of the evils of a segregated society written for young readers.

Emily Dickinson

Emily Dickinson is ranked as one of America's greatest poets. Dickinson's poetry is highly formal, her language both subtle and creative, and it reflects the quiet life she led. Dickinson's topics include death, art, love, pain, and betrayal, all couched in her wonderful poetic language. She wrote more than 1,800 poems, yet only ten are known to have been published in her lifetime. Her fame has grown through the generations, and she is at last recognized as a poetic genius.
Born in Amherst, Massachusetts, in 1830, she was educated at Mt. Holyoke seminary. She returned to Amherst and went into virtual seclusion in her parents' home. She saw very few people socially and rarely left the house. Despite this isolation, Dickinson's work is vibrant and alive, reflecting her keen observation of the world. Dickinson is a true American literary voice, rivaling Walt Whitman. She died in Amherst in 1886.

Robert Louis Stevenson

Robert Louis Stevenson was a Scottish essayist, novelist, poet, and short-story writer. After writing for weeklies for a few years, his Treasure Island (1883) brought him acclaim and wealth. Stevenson followed this success with Kidnapped (1886), The Strange Case of Dr. Jekyll and Mr. Hyde (1886), and The Master of Ballantrae (1889), all critical and financial successes. Stevenson also wrote a book of verse for children, A Child's Garden of Verses (1885). His swashbuckling tales and colorful language engaged the fancy of the public, and he retired a wealthy man. Stevenson was born in Edinburgh in 1850 and educated in law. His life was tainted by chronic tuberculosis, and he sought cures and more healthy climates all over the world. Stevenson finally found the relief he sought in Samoa, where he settled and lived the last years of his life. He died there in 1894, at the young age of 44.

Rudyard Kipling

Kipling, the favorite writer of the British Empire, was a novelist, poet, and short-fiction writer of great skill. His novels of British imperialism, such as Kim (1901), carved a unique literary niche for Kipling. His poetry was much beloved; outstanding examples are "Gunga Din," "Mandalay," and "Danny Deever." Kipling's story collections for children include The Jungle Book (1894) and Just So Stories (1902). Kipling's descriptions of British colonial life became a window for the world to understand the glory and excesses of the empire.
Kipling was born in Bombay in 1865 and educated in England. He returned to India for several years, working as a journalist and fledgling poet. Returning to England, his prose collection captured the fancy of the nation. Kipling lived for four productive years in Vermont and then went home for good. The first English writer to win a Nobel Prize for Literature, he died in England in 1936.

Robert Frost

Robert Frost, American poet, is remembered as a master of the technical aspects of poetry while remaining true to his New England heritage. Frost will always be remembered for his masterful simplicity in such poems as "Stopping By the Woods on a Snowy Evening" (1923) and "The Road Not Taken" (1916). While living in England before World War I, Frost published two collections of poetry. Returning to New England, he published a number of anthologies, including Complete Poems (1945), West Running Brook (1928), A Witness Tree (1942), and In the Clearing (1962). Frost was born in California in 1874 and was educated at Dartmouth College and Harvard. He received the Pulitzer Prize four times and capped his career by reading "The Gift Outright" at the inaugural of John Kennedy in 1961. Frost died in 1963.

Examples and illustrations

Examples are a common method of development and may be effectively used when a reader may ask, "For example?" Examples are selected instances, not an inclusive catalog. They may be used to suggest the validity of topic sentences. Illustrations are extended examples, sometimes presented in story form for interest. They usually require several sentences each, so they are used sparingly. Well-selected illustrations can be a colorful and vivid way of developing a point. Stories that command reader interest, developed in a story form, can be powerful methods of emphasizing key points in an essay. Stories and illustrations should be specific and relate directly to a point or points being made in the text. They allow more colorful language and instill a sense of human interest in a subject. Used judiciously, illustrations and stories are excellent devices.

Visual elements in documents

Visual elements such as charts, graphs, tables, photographs, maps, and diagrams are useful in conveying information vividly and in a summary form.
Flow charts and pie charts are useful in helping readers follow a process or showing numerical information in graphic style. Tables are less stimulating but offer devices for summarizing information. Diagrams are useful and sometimes necessary in scientific writing, to explain chemical formulas for example.
Visual elements may be placed in a document close to the textual discussion, or put in an appendix, labeled, and referred to in a text. Sometimes page layout makes it difficult to position visuals in optimum proximity to the corresponding text. In these cases visuals may be placed later in the text, and readers told where they can find it. Software may be used to help the text flow around the visual for maximum impact.

Evaluating student writing

The evaluation of student writing should be structured to include three basic goals:
- To provide students a description of what they are doing when they respond
- To provide a pathway for potential improvement
- To help students learn to evaluate themselves

To fulfill these goals, it is necessary for the concept of evaluation to be broadened beyond correcting or judging students. Any teacher response to a student's response should be considered part of the evaluation. In responding to student's responses, a teacher may use written or taped comments, dialogue with students, or conferencing between teacher and students to discuss classroom performance. Students may be asked to evaluate themselves and a teacher, and students can review past progress and plan directions for potential improvement.

Literary tests and assessments

Literary tests are measures of a student's individual performance. Literary assessments are measures of performance of a group of students without reference to individuals. Tests take into consideration what the teacher has taught the students, whereas assessments do not.
For either tests or assessments, the teacher needs a clear purpose on which to base questions or activities. Students should be told of the purpose of the tests or assessments so they will know what to expect. Tests should be used sparingly as one tool among many that can be used to evaluate students. Tests should encourage students on formulation of responses rather than rote answers. They should evaluate students on the basis of their responses rather than correct answers. Improvement over time may be noted and the students praised for specific responses.

Standardized achievement tests

These multiple-choice tests measure students' ability to understand text passages or apply literary concepts to texts. Although these tests are widely used, they have many limitations. They tend to be based on a simplistic model that ignores the complex nature of a reader's engagement with a text. These tests also do not measure students' articulation of responses. The purpose of these tests is to rank students in group norms so that half the students are below the norm. To accurately measure a student's abilities, teachers should employ open-ended written or oral-response activities. In developing such tests, teachers must know what specific response patterns they wish to measure. The steps involved in measuring these response patterns must be clearly outlined. Teachers may wish to design questions that encourage personal expressions of responses. This would obviate the pitfall of testing primarily facts about literature rather than how students relate and use this information to engage texts.

Mathematics

Numbers and their Classifications

Numbers are the basic building blocks of mathematics. Specific features of numbers are identified by the following terms:

Integers – The set of whole positive and negative numbers, including zero. Integers do not include fractions ($\frac{1}{3}$), decimals (0.56), or mixed numbers ($7\frac{3}{4}$).

Prime number – A whole number greater than 1 that has only two factors, itself and 1; that is, a number that can be divided evenly only by 1 and itself. 2, 3, 5, 7, 11, 13, 17, 19, 23, 29, 31, 37 ...

Composite number – A whole number greater than 1 that has more than two different factors; in other words, any whole number that is not a prime number. For example: The composite number 8 has the factors of 1, 2, 4, and 8.

Even number – Any integer that can be divided by 2 without leaving a remainder. For example: 2, 4, 6, 8, and so on.

Odd number – Any integer that cannot be divided evenly by 2. For example: 3, 5, 7, 9, and so on.

Decimal number – a number that uses a decimal point to show the part of the number that is less than one. Example: 1.234.

Decimal point – a symbol used to separate the ones place from the tenths place in decimals or dollars from cents in currency.

Decimal place – the position of a number to the right of the decimal point. In the decimal 0.123, the 1 is in the first place to the right of the decimal point, indicating tenths; the 2 is in the second place, indicating hundredths; and the 3 is in the third place, indicating thousandths.

The decimal, or base 10, system is a number system that uses ten different digits (0, 1, 2, 3, 4, 5, 6, 7, 8, 9). An example of a number system that uses something other than ten digits is the binary, or base 2, number system, used by computers, which uses only the numbers 0 and 1. It is thought that the decimal system originated because people had only their 10 fingers for counting.

Rational, irrational, and real numbers can be described as follows:

Rational numbers include all integers, decimals, and fractions. Any terminating or repeating decimal number is a rational number.

Irrational numbers cannot be written as fractions or decimals because the number of decimal places is infinite and there is no recurring pattern of digits within the number. For example, pi (π) begins with 3.141592 and continues without terminating or repeating, so pi is an irrational number.

Real numbers are the set of all rational and irrational numbers.

Operations

There are four basic mathematical operations:

Addition increases the value of one quantity by the value of another quantity. Example: $2 + 4 = 6$; $8 + 9 = 17$. The result is called the sum. With addition, the order does not matter. $4 + 2 = 2 + 4$.

Subtraction is the opposite operation to addition; it decreases the value of one quantity by the value of another quantity. Example: $6 - 4 = 2; 17 - 8 = 9$. The result is called the difference. Note that with subtraction, the order does matter. $6 - 4 \neq 4 - 6$.

Multiplication can be thought of as repeated addition. One number tells how many times to add the other number to itself. Example: 3×2 (three times two) $= 2 + 2 + 2 = 6$. With multiplication, the order does not matter. $2 \times 3 = 3 \times 2$ or $3 + 3 = 2 + 2 + 2$.

Division is the opposite operation to multiplication; one number tells us how many parts to divide the other number into. Example: $20 \div 4 = 5$; if 20 is split into 4 equal parts, each part is 5. With division, the order of the numbers does matter. $20 \div 4 \neq 4 \div 20$.

An exponent is a superscript number placed next to another number at the top right. It indicates how many times the base number is to be multiplied by itself. Exponents provide a shorthand way to write what would be a longer mathematical expression. Example: $a^2 = a \times a; 2^4 = 2 \times 2 \times 2 \times 2$. A number with an exponent of 2 is said to be "squared," while a number with an exponent of 3 is said to be "cubed." The value of a number raised to an exponent is called its power. So, 8^4 is read as "8 to the 4th power," or "8 raised to the power of 4." A negative exponent is the same as the reciprocal of a positive exponent. Example: $a^{-2} = \dfrac{1}{a^2}$.

Parentheses are used to designate which operations should be done first when there are multiple operations. Example: 4 – (2 + 1) = 1; the parentheses tell us that we must add 2 and 1, and then subtract the sum from 4, rather than subtracting 2 from 4 and then adding 1 (this would give us an answer of 3).

Order of Operations is a set of rules that dictates the order in which we must perform each operation in an expression so that we will evaluate at accurately. If we have an expression that includes multiple different operations, Order of Operations tells us which operations to do first. The most common mnemonic for Order of Operations is PEMDAS, or "Please Excuse My Dear Aunt Sally." PEMDAS stands for Parentheses, Exponents, Multiplication, Division, Addition, Subtraction. It is important to understand that multiplication and division have equal precedence, as do addition and subtraction, so those pairs of operations are simply worked from left to right in order.

Example: Evaluate the expression $5 + 20 \div 4 \times (2 + 3)^2 - 6$ using the correct order of operations.
P: Perform the operations inside the parentheses, $(2 + 3) = 5$.
E: Simplify the exponents, $(5)^2 = 25$.
The equation now looks like this: $5 + 20 \div 4 \times 25 - 6$.
MD: Perform multiplication and division from left to right, $20 \div 4 = 5$; then $5 \times 25 = 125$.
The equation now looks like this: $5 + 125 - 6$.
AS: Perform addition and subtraction from left to right, $5 + 125 = 130$; then $130 - 6 = 124$.

The laws of exponents are as follows:
1)   Any number to the power of 1 is equal to itself: $a^1 = a$.
2)   The number 1 raised to any power is equal to 1: $1^n = 1$.
3)   Any number raised to the power of 0 is equal to 1: $a^0 = 1$.
4)   Add exponents to multiply powers of the same base number: $a^n \times a^m = a^{n+m}$.
5)   Subtract exponents to divide powers of the same number; that is $a^n \div a^m = a^{n-m}$.
6)   Multiply exponents to raise a power to a power: $(a^n)^m = a^{n \times m}$.

7)   If multiplied or divided numbers inside parentheses are collectively raised to a power, this is the same as each individual term being raised to that power: $(a \times b)^n = a^n \times b^n$; $(a \div b)^n = a^n \div b^n$.

Note: Exponents do not have to be integers. Fractional or decimal exponents follow all the rules above as well. Example: $5^{\frac{1}{4}} \times 5^{\frac{3}{4}} = 5^{\frac{1}{4}+\frac{3}{4}} = 5^1 = 5$.

A root, such as a square root, is another way of writing a fractional exponent. Instead of using a superscript, roots use the radical symbol ($\sqrt{}$) to indicate the operation. A radical will have a number underneath the bar, and may sometimes have a number in the upper left: $\sqrt[n]{a}$, read as "the nth root of a." The relationship between radical notation and exponent notation can be described by this equation: $\sqrt[n]{a} = a^{\frac{1}{n}}$. The two special cases of $n = 2$ and $n = 3$ are called square roots and cube roots. If there is no number to the upper left, it is understood to be a square root ($n = 2$). Nearly all of the roots you encounter will be square roots. A square root is the same as a number raised to the one-half power. When we say that a is the square root of b ($a = \sqrt{b}$), we mean that a multiplied by itself equals b: ($a \times a = b$).

A perfect square is a number that has an integer for its square root. There are 10 perfect squares from 1 to 100: 1, 4, 9, 16, 25, 36, 49, 64, 81, 100 (the squares of integers 1 through 10).

Scientific notation is a way of writing large numbers in a shorter form. The form $a \times 10^n$ is used in scientific notation, where a is greater than or equal to 1, but less than 10, and n is the number of places the decimal must move to get from the original number to a. Example: The number 230,400,000 is cumbersome to write. To write the value in scientific notation, place a decimal point between the first and second numbers, and include all digits through the last non-zero digit ($a = 2.304$). To find the appropriate power of 10, count the number of places the decimal point had to move ($n = 8$). The number is positive if the decimal moved to the left, and negative if it moved to the right. We can then write 230,400,000 as 2.304×10^8. If we look instead at the number 0.00002304, we have the same value for a, but this time the decimal moved 5 places to the right ($n = -5$). Thus, 0.00002304 can be written as 2.304×10^{-5}. Using this notation makes it simple to compare very large or very small numbers. By comparing exponents, it is easy to see that 3.28×10^4 is smaller than 1.51×10^5, because 4 is less than 5.

Factors and Multiples

Factors are numbers that are multiplied together to obtain a product. For example, in the equation $2 \times 3 = 6$, the numbers 2 and 3 are factors. A prime number has only two factors (1 and itself), but other numbers can have many factors.

A common factor is a number that divides exactly into two or more other numbers. For example, the factors of 12 are 1, 2, 3, 4, 6, and 12, while the factors of 15 are 1, 3, 5, and 15. The common factors of 12 and 15 are 1 and 3.

A prime factor is also a prime number. Therefore, the prime factors of 12 are 1, 2, and 3. For 15, the prime factors are 1, 3, and 5.

The greatest common factor (GCF) is the largest number that is a factor of two or more numbers. For example, the factors of 15 are 1, 3, 5, and 15; the factors of 35 are 1, 5, 7, and 35. Therefore, the greatest common factor of 15 and 35 is 5.

The least common multiple (LCM) is the smallest number that is a multiple of two or more numbers. For example, the multiples of 3 include 3, 6, 9, 12, 15, etc.; the multiples of 5 include 5, 10, 15, 20, etc. Therefore, the least common multiple of 3 and 5 is 15.

Fractions, Percentages, and Related Concepts

A fraction is a number that is expressed as one integer written above another integer, with a dividing line between them $\left(\frac{x}{y}\right)$. It represents the quotient of the two numbers "x divided by y." It can also be thought of as x out of y equal parts.

The top number of a fraction is called the numerator, and it represents the number of parts under consideration. The 1 in $\frac{1}{4}$ means that 1 part out of the whole is being considered in the calculation. The bottom number of a fraction is called the denominator, and it represents the total number of equal parts. The 4 in $\frac{1}{4}$ means that the whole consists of 4 equal parts. A fraction cannot have a denominator of zero; this is referred to as "undefined."

Fractions can be manipulated, without changing the value of the fraction, by multiplying or dividing (but not adding or subtracting) both the numerator and denominator by the same number. If you divide both numbers by a common factor, you are reducing or simplifying the fraction. Two fractions that have the same value, but are expressed differently are known as equivalent fractions. For example, $\frac{2}{10}, \frac{3}{15}, \frac{4}{20}$, and $\frac{5}{25}$ are all equivalent fractions. They can also all be reduced or simplified to $\frac{1}{5}$.

When two fractions are manipulated so that they have the same denominator, this is known as finding a common denominator. The number chosen to be that common denominator should be the least common multiple of the two original denominators. Example: $\frac{3}{4}$ and $\frac{5}{6}$; the least common multiple of 4 and 6 is 12. Manipulating to achieve the common denominator: $\frac{3}{4} = \frac{9}{12}; \frac{5}{6} = \frac{10}{12}$.

If two fractions have a common denominator, they can be added or subtracted simply by adding or subtracting the two numerators and retaining the same denominator. Example: $\frac{1}{2} + \frac{1}{4} = \frac{2}{4} + \frac{1}{4} = \frac{3}{4}$. If the two fractions do not already have the same denominator, one or both of them must be manipulated to achieve a common denominator before they can be added or subtracted.

Two fractions can be multiplied by multiplying the two numerators to find the new numerator and the two denominators to find the new denominator. Example: $\frac{1}{3} \times \frac{2}{3} = \frac{1 \times 2}{3 \times 3} = \frac{2}{9}$.

Two fractions can be divided flipping the numerator and denominator of the second fraction and then proceeding as though it were a multiplication. Example: $\frac{2}{3} \div \frac{3}{4} = \frac{2}{3} \times \frac{4}{3} = \frac{8}{9}$.

A fraction whose denominator is greater than its numerator is known as a proper fraction, while a fraction whose numerator is greater than its denominator is known as an improper fraction. Proper fractions have values less than one and improper fractions have values greater than one.

A mixed number is a number that contains both an integer and a fraction. Any improper fraction can be rewritten as a mixed number. Example: $\frac{8}{3} = \frac{6}{3} + \frac{2}{3} = 2 + \frac{2}{3} = 2\frac{2}{3}$. Similarly, any mixed number can be rewritten as an improper fraction. Example: $1\frac{3}{5} = 1 + \frac{3}{5} = \frac{5}{5} + \frac{3}{5} = \frac{8}{5}$.

Percentages can be thought of as fractions that are based on a whole of 100; that is, one whole is equal to 100%. The word percent means "per hundred." Fractions can be expressed as percents by finding equivalent fractions with a denomination of 100. Example: $\frac{7}{10} = \frac{70}{100} = 70\%$; $\frac{1}{4} = \frac{25}{100} = 25\%$.

To express a percentage as a fraction, divide the percentage number by 100 and reduce the fraction to its simplest possible terms. Example: $60\% = \frac{60}{100} = \frac{3}{5}$; $96\% = \frac{96}{100} = \frac{24}{25}$.

Converting decimals to percentages and percentages to decimals is as simple as moving the decimal point. To convert from a decimal to a percent, move the decimal point two places to the right. To convert from a percent to a decimal, move it two places to the left. Example: 0.23 = 23%; 5.34 = 534%; 0.007 = 0.7%; 700% = 7.00; 86% = 0.86; 0.15% = 0.0015.

It may be helpful to remember that the percentage number will always be larger than the equivalent decimal number.

A percentage problem can be presented three main ways: (1) Find what percentage of some number another number is. Example: What percentage of 40 is 8? (2) Find what number is some percentage of a given number. Example: What number is 20% of 40? (3) Find what number another number is a given percentage of. Example: What number is 8 20% of? The three components in all of these cases are the same: a whole (W), a part (P), and a percentage (%). These are related by the equation: $P = W \times \%$. This is the form of the equation you would use to solve problems of type (2). To solve types (1) and (3), you would use these two forms: $\% = \frac{P}{W}$ and $W = \frac{P}{\%}$.

The thing that frequently makes percentage problems difficult is that they are most often also word problems, so a large part of solving them is figuring out which quantities are what. Example: In a school cafeteria, 7 students choose pizza, 9 choose hamburgers, and 4 choose tacos. Find the percentage that chooses tacos. To find the whole, you must first add all of the parts: 7 + 9 + 4 = 20. The percentage can then be found by dividing the part by the whole ($\% = \frac{P}{W}$): $\frac{4}{20} = \frac{20}{100} = 20\%$.

A ratio is a comparison of two quantities in a particular order. Example: If there are 14 computers in a lab, and the class has 20 students, there is a student to computer ratio of 20 to 14, commonly written as 20:14. Ratios are normally reduced to their smallest whole number representation, so 20:14 would be reduced to 10:7 by dividing both sides by 2.

A proportion is a relationship between two quantities that dictates how one changes when the other changes. A direct proportion describes a relationship in which a quantity increases by a set amount for every increase in the other quantity, or decreases by that same amount for every decrease in the other quantity. Example: Assuming a constant driving speed, the time required for a car trip increases as the distance of the trip increases. The distance to be traveled and the time required to travel are directly proportional.

Inverse proportion is a relationship in which an increase in one quantity is accompanied by a decrease in the other, or vice versa. Example: the time required for a car trip decreases as the speed increases, and increases as the speed decreases, so the time required is inversely proportional to the speed of the car.

Geometry concepts

Below are some terms that are commonly used in geometric studies. Most of these concepts are foundational to geometry, so understanding them is a necessary first step to studying geometry.

A point is a fixed location in space; has no size or dimensions; commonly represented by a dot.

A line is a set of points that extends infinitely in two opposite directions. It has length, but no width or depth. A line can be defined by any two distinct points that it contains. A line segment is a portion of a line that has definite endpoints. A ray is a portion of a line that extends from a single point on that line in one direction along the line. It has a definite beginning, but no ending.

A plane is a two-dimensional flat surface defined by three non-collinear points. A plane extends an infinite distance in all directions in those two dimensions. It contains an infinite number of points, parallel lines and segments, intersecting lines and segments, as well as parallel or intersecting rays. A plane will never contain a three-dimensional figure or skew lines. Two given planes will either be parallel or they will intersect to form a line. A plane may intersect a circular conic surface, such as a cone, to form conic sections, such as the parabola, hyperbola, circle or ellipse.

Perpendicular lines are lines that intersect at right angles. They are represented by the symbol ⊥.

The shortest distance from a line to a point not on the line is a perpendicular segment from the point to the line.

Parallel lines are lines in the same plane that have no points in common and never meet. It is possible for lines to be in different planes, have no points in common, and never meet, but they are not parallel because they are in different planes.

A bisector is a line or line segment that divides another line segment into two equal lengths. A perpendicular bisector of a line segment is composed of points that are equidistant from the endpoints of the segment it is dividing.

Intersecting lines are lines that have exactly one point in common. Concurrent lines are multiple lines that intersect at a single point.

A transversal is a line that intersects at least two other lines, which may or may not be parallel to one another. A transversal that intersects parallel lines is a common occurrence in geometry.

Angles

An angle is formed when two lines or line segments meet at a common point. It may be a common starting point for a pair of segments or rays, or it may be the intersection of lines. Angles are represented by the symbol ∠.

The vertex is the point at which two segments or rays meet to form an angle. If the angle is formed by intersecting rays, lines, and/or line segments, the vertex is the point at which four angles are formed. The pairs of angles opposite one another are called vertical angles, and their measures are equal. In the figure below, angles ABC and DBE are congruent, as are angles ABD and CBE.

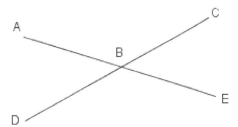

An acute angle is an angle with a degree measure less than 90°.
A right angle is an angle with a degree measure of exactly 90°.
An obtuse angle is an angle with a degree measure greater than 90° but less than 180°.
A straight angle is an angle with a degree measure of exactly 180°. This is also a semicircle.
A reflex angle is an angle with a degree measure greater than 180° but less than 360°.
A full angle is an angle with a degree measure of exactly 360°.

Two angles whose sum is exactly 90° are said to be complementary. The two angles may or may not be adjacent. In a right triangle, the two acute angles are complementary.

Two angles whose sum is exactly 180° are said to be supplementary. The two angles may or may not be adjacent. Two intersecting lines always form two pairs of supplementary angles. Adjacent supplementary angles will always form a straight line.

Two angles that have the same vertex and share a side are said to be adjacent. Vertical angles are not adjacent because they share a vertex but no common side.

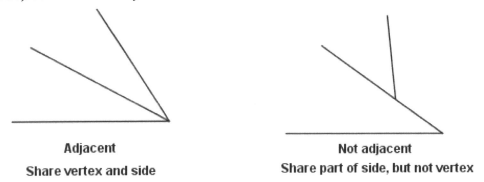

| **Adjacent** | **Not adjacent** |
| **Share vertex and side** | **Share part of side, but not vertex** |

When two parallel lines are cut by a transversal, the angles that are between the two parallel lines are interior angles. In the diagram below, angles 3, 4, 5, and 6 are interior angles.

When two parallel lines are cut by a transversal, the angles that are outside the parallel lines are exterior angles. In the diagram below, angles 1, 2, 7, and 8 are exterior angles.

When two parallel lines are cut by a transversal, the angles that are in the same position relative to the transversal and a parallel line are corresponding angles. The diagram below has four pairs of corresponding angles: angles 1 and 5; angles 2 and 6; angles 3 and 7; and angles 4 and 8. Corresponding angles formed by parallel lines are congruent.

When two parallel lines are cut by a transversal, the two interior angles that are on opposite sides of the transversal are called alternate interior angles. In the diagram below, there are two pairs of alternate interior angles: angles 3 and 6, and angles 4 and 5. Alternate interior angles formed by parallel lines are congruent.

When two parallel lines are cut by a transversal, the two exterior angles that are on opposite sides of the transversal are called alternate exterior angles. In the diagram below, there are two pairs of alternate exterior angles: angles 1 and 8, and angles 2 and 7. Alternate exterior angles formed by parallel lines are congruent.

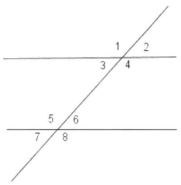

Circles

The center is the single point inside the circle that is equidistant from every point on the circle. (Point O in the diagram below.)

The radius is a line segment that joins the center of the circle and any one point on the circle. All radii of a circle are equal. (Segments OX, OY, and OZ in the diagram below.)

The diameter is a line segment that passes through the center of the circle and has both endpoints on the circle. The length of the diameter is exactly twice the length of the radius. (Segment XZ in the diagram below.)

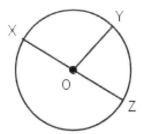

A circle is inscribed in a polygon if each of the sides of the polygon is tangent to the circle. A polygon is inscribed in a circle if each of the vertices of the polygon lies on the circle.

A circle is circumscribed about a polygon if each of the vertices of the polygon lies on the circle. A polygon is circumscribed about the circle if each of the sides of the polygon is tangent to the circle.

If one figure is inscribed in another, then the other figure is circumscribed about the first figure.

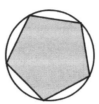

Circle circumscribed about a pentagon
Pentagon inscribed in a circle

Polygons

A polygon is a planar shape formed from line segments called sides that are joined together at points called vertices (singular: vertex). Specific polygons are named by the number of angles or sides they have. Regular polygons are polygons whose sides are all equal and whose angles are all congruent.

An interior angle is any of the angles inside a polygon where two sides meet at a vertex. The sum of the interior angles of a polygon is dependent only on the number of sides. For example, all 5-sided polygons have interior angles that sum to 540°, regardless of the particular shape.
A diagonal is a line that joins two nonconsecutive vertices of a polygon. The number of diagonals that can be drawn on an n-sided polygon is $d = \frac{n(n-3)}{2}$.

The following list presents several different types of polygons:
Triangle – 3 sides
Quadrilateral – 4 sides
Pentagon – 5 sides
Hexagon – 6 sides
Heptagon – 7 sides
Octagon – 8 sides
Nonagon – 9 sides
Decagon – 10 sides
Dodecagon – 12 sides
More generally, an n-gon is a polygon that has n angles and n sides.

The sum of the interior angles of an n-sided polygon is $(n - 2)180°$. For example, in a triangle n = 3, so the sum of the interior angles is $(3 - 2)180° = 180°$. In a quadrilateral, n = 4, and the sum of the angles is $(4 - 2)180° = 360°$. The sum of the interior angles of a polygon is equal to the sum of the interior angles of any other polygon with the same number of sides.

Below are descriptions for several common quadrilaterals. Recall that a quadrilateral is a four-sided polygon.

Trapezoid – quadrilateral with exactly one pair of parallel sides (opposite one another); in an isosceles trapezoid, the two non-parallel sides have equal length and both pairs of non-opposite angles are congruent

Parallelogram – quadrilateral with two pairs of parallel sides (opposite one another), and two pairs of congruent angles (opposite one another)
Rhombus – parallelogram with four equal sides
Rectangle – parallelogram with four congruent angles (right angles)
Square – parallelogram with four equal sides and four congruent angles (right angles)

Triangles

A triangle is a polygon with three sides and three angles. Triangles can be classified according to the length of their sides or magnitude of their angles.

An acute triangle is a triangle whose three angles are all less than 90°. If two of the angles are equal, the acute triangle is also an isosceles triangle. If the three angles are all equal, the acute triangle is also an equilateral triangle.

A right triangle is a triangle with exactly one angle equal to 90°. All right triangles follow the Pythagorean Theorem. A right triangle can never be acute or obtuse.

An obtuse triangle is a triangle with exactly one angle greater than 90°. The other two angles may or may not be equal. If the two remaining angles are equal, the obtuse triangle is also an isosceles triangle.

An equilateral triangle is a triangle with three congruent sides. An equilateral triangle will also have three congruent angles, each 60°. All equilateral triangles are also acute triangles.

An isosceles triangle is a triangle with two congruent sides. An isosceles triangle will also have two congruent angles opposite the two congruent sides.

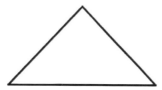

A scalene triangle is a triangle with no congruent sides. A scalene triangle will also have three angles of different measures. The angle with the largest measure is opposite the longest side, and the angle with the smallest measure is opposite the shortest side.

The Triangle Inequality Theorem states that the sum of the measures of any two sides of a triangle is always greater than the measure of the third side. If the sum of the measures of two sides were equal to the third side, a triangle would be impossible because the two sides would lie flat across the third side and there would be no vertex. If the sum of the measures of two of the sides was less than the third side, a closed figure would be impossible because the two shortest sides would never meet.

Similar triangles are triangles whose corresponding angles are congruent to one another. Their corresponding sides may or may not be equal, but they are proportional to one another. Since the angles in a triangle always sum to 180°, it is only necessary to determine that two pairs of corresponding angles are congruent, since the third will be also in that case.

Congruent triangles are similar triangles whose corresponding sides are all equal. Congruent triangles can be made to fit on top of one another by rotation, reflection, and/or translation. When trying to determine whether two triangles are congruent, there are several criteria that can be used.

Side-side-side (SSS): if all three sides of one triangle are equal to all three sides of another triangle, they are congruent by SSS.
Side-angle-side (SAS): if two sides and the adjoining angle in one triangle are equal to two sides and the adjoining angle of another triangle, they are congruent by SAS.
Additionally, if two triangles can be shown to be similar, then there need only be one pair of corresponding equal sides to show congruence.

One of the most important theorems in geometry is the Pythagorean Theorem. Named after the sixth-century Greek mathematician Pythagoras, this theorem states that, for a right triangle, the square of the hypotenuse (the longest side of the triangle, always opposite the right angle) is equal to the sum of the squares of the other two sides. Written symbolically, the Pythagorean Theorem can be expressed as $a^2 + b^2 = c^2$, where c is the hypotenuse and a and b are the remaining two sides.

The theorem is most commonly used to find the length of an unknown side of a right triangle, given the lengths of the other two sides. For example, given that the hypotenuse of a right triangle is 5 and one side is 3, the other side can be found using the formula: $a^2 + b^2 = c^2$, $3^2 + b^2 = 5^2$, $9 + b^2 = 25$, $b^2 = 25 - 9 = 16$, $b = \sqrt{16} = 4$.

The theorem can also be used "in reverse" to show that when the square of one side of a triangle is equal to the sum of the squares of the other two sides, the triangle must be a right triangle.

The Law of Sines states that $\frac{\sin A}{a} = \frac{\sin B}{b} = \frac{\sin C}{c}$, where A, B, and C are the angles of a triangle, and a, b, and c are the sides opposite their respective angles. This formula will work with all triangles, not just right triangles.

The Law of Cosines is given by the formula $c^2 = a^2 + b^2 - 2ab(\cos C)$, where a, b, and c are the sides of a triangle, and C is the angle opposite side c. This formula is similar to the Pythagorean Theorem, but unlike the Pythagorean Theorem, it can be used on any triangle.

Symmetry

Symmetry is a property of a shape in which the shape can be transformed by either reflection or rotation without losing its original shape and orientation. A shape that has reflection symmetry can be reflected across a line with the result being the same shape as before the reflection. A line of symmetry divides a shape into two parts, with each part being a mirror image of the other. A shape can have more than one line of symmetry. A circle, for instance, has an infinite number of lines of symmetry. When reflection symmetry is extended to three-dimensional space, it is taken to describe a solid that can be divided into mirror image parts by a plane of symmetry.

Rotational symmetry describes a shape that can be rotated about a point and achieve its original shape and orientation with less than a 360° rotation. When rotational symmetry is extended to three-dimensional space, it describes a solid that can be rotated about a line with the same conditions. Many shapes have both reflection and rotational symmetry.

Area formulas

Rectangle: $A = wl$, where w is the width and l is the length
Square: $A = s^2$, where s is the length of a side.
Triangle: $A = \frac{1}{2}bh$, where b is the length of one side (base) and h is the distance from that side to the opposite vertex measured perpendicularly (height).
Parallelogram: $A = bh$, where b is the length of one side (base) and h is the perpendicular distance between that side and its parallel side (height).
Trapezoid: $A = \frac{1}{2}(b_1 + b_2)h$, where b_1 and b_2 are the lengths of the two parallel sides (bases), and h is the perpendicular distance between them (height).
Circle: $A = \pi r^2$, where π is the mathematical constant approximately equal to 3.14 and r is the distance from the center of the circle to any point on the circle (radius).

Volume Formulas

For some of these shapes, it is necessary to find the area of the base polygon before the volume of the solid can be found. This base area is represented in the volume equations as B.
Pyramid – consists of a polygon base, and triangles connecting each side of that polygon to a vertex. The volume can be calculated as $V = \frac{1}{3}Bh$, where h is the distance between the vertex and the base polygon, measured perpendicularly.
Prism – consists of two identical polygon bases, attached to one another on corresponding sides by parallelograms. The volume can be calculated as $V = Bh$, where h is the perpendicular distance between the two bases.
Cube – a special type of prism in which the two bases are the same shape as the side faces. All faces are squares. The volume can be calculated as $V = s^3$, where s is the length of any side.

Sphere – a round solid consisting of one continuous, uniformly-curved surface. The volume can be calculated as $V = \frac{4}{3}\pi r^3$, where r is the distance from the center of the sphere to any point on the surface (radius).

Probability

Probability is a branch of statistics that deals with the likelihood of something taking place. One classic example is a coin toss. There are only two possible results: heads or tails. The likelihood, or probability, that the coin will land as heads is 1 out of 2 (1/2, 0.5, 50%). Tails has the same probability. Another common example is a 6-sided die roll. There are six possible results from rolling a single die, each with an equal chance of happening, so the probability of any given number coming up is 1 out of 6.

Terms frequently used in probability:
Event – a situation that produces results of some sort (a coin toss)
Compound event – event that involves two or more independent events (rolling a pair of dice; taking the sum)
Outcome – a possible result in an experiment or event (heads, tails)
Desired outcome (or success) – an outcome that meets a particular set of criteria (a roll of 1 or 2 if we are looking for numbers less than 3)
Independent events – two or more events whose outcomes do not affect one another (two coins tossed at the same time)
Dependent events – two or more events whose outcomes affect one another (two cards drawn consecutively from the same deck)
Certain outcome – probability of outcome is 100% or 1
Impossible outcome – probability of outcome is 0% or 0
Mutually exclusive outcomes – two or more outcomes whose criteria cannot all be satisfied in a single event (a coin coming up heads and tails on the same toss)

Probability is the likelihood of a certain outcome occurring for a given event. The **theoretical probability** can usually be determined without actually performing the event. The likelihood of a outcome occurring, or the probability of an outcome occurring, is given by the formula
$$P(A) = \frac{\text{Number of acceptable outcomes}}{\text{Number of possible outcomes}}$$
where $P(A)$ is the probability of an outcome A occurring, and each outcome is just as likely to occur as any other outcome. If each outcome has the same probability of occurring as every other possible outcome, the outcomes are said to be equally likely to occur. The total number of acceptable outcomes must be less than or equal to the total number of possible outcomes. If the two are equal, then the outcome is certain to occur and the probability is 1. If the number of acceptable outcomes is zero, then the outcome is impossible and the probability is 0.
Example:
There are 20 marbles in a bag and 5 are red. The theoretical probability of randomly selecting a red marble is 5 out of 20, (5/20 = 1/4, 0.25, or 25%).

When trying to calculate the probability of an event using the $\frac{desired\ outcomes}{total\ outcomes}$ formula, you may frequently find that there are too many outcomes to individually count them. Permutation and combination formulas offer a shortcut to counting outcomes. A permutation is an arrangement of a specific number of a set of objects in a specific order. The number of **permutations** of r items given a set of n items can be calculated as $_nP_r = \frac{n!}{(n-r)!}$. Combinations are similar to permutations, except there are no restrictions regarding the order of the elements. While ABC is considered a different permutation than BCA, ABC and BCA are considered the same combination. The number of **combinations** of r items given a set of n items can be calculated as $_nC_r = \frac{n!}{r!(n-r)!}$ or $_nC_r = \frac{_nP_r}{r!}$. Example: Suppose you want to calculate how many different 5-card hands can be drawn from a deck of 52 cards. This is a combination since the order of the cards in a hand does not matter. There are 52 cards available, and 5 to be selected. Thus, the number of different hands is $_{52}C_5 = \frac{52!}{5! \times 47!} = 2,598,960$.

Sometimes it may be easier to calculate the possibility of something not happening, or the **complement of an event**. Represented by the symbol $\bar{A}$, the complement of A is the probability that event A does not happen. When you know the probability of event A occurring, you can use the formula $P(\bar{A}) = 1 - P(A)$, where $P(\bar{A})$ is the probability of event A not occurring, and $P(A)$ is the probability of event A occurring.

The **addition rule** for probability is used for finding the probability of a compound event. Use the formula $P(A \text{ or } B) = P(A) + P(B) - P(A \text{ and } B)$, where $P(A \text{ and } B)$ is the probability of both events occurring to find the probability of a compound event. The probability of both events occurring at the same time must be subtracted to eliminate any overlap in the first two probabilities.

Conditional probability is the probability of an event occurring once another event has already occurred. Given event A and dependent event B, the probability of event B occurring when event A has already occurred is represented by the notation $P(A|B)$. To find the probability of event B occurring, take into account the fact that event A has already occurred and adjust the total number of possible outcomes. For example, suppose you have ten balls numbered 1–10 and you want ball number 7 to be pulled in two pulls. On the first pull, the probability of getting the 7 is $\frac{1}{10}$ because there is one ball with a 7 on it and 10 balls to choose from. Assuming the first pull did not yield a 7, the probability of pulling a 7 on the second pull is now $\frac{1}{9}$ because there are only 9 balls remaining for the second pull.

The **multiplication rule** can be used to find the probability of two independent events occurring using the formula $P(A \text{ and } B) = P(A) \times P(B)$, where $P(A \text{ and } B)$ is the probability of two independent events occurring, $P(A)$ is the probability of the first event occurring, and $P(B)$ is the probability of the second event occurring.

The multiplication rule can also be used to find the probability of two dependent events occurring using the formula $P(A \text{ and } B) = P(A) \times P(B|A)$, where $P(A \text{ and } B)$ is the probability of two dependent events occurring and $P(B|A)$ is the probability of the second event occurring after the first event has already occurred.

Before using the multiplication rule, you MUST first determine whether the two events are dependent or independent.

Use a combination of the multiplication rule and the rule of complements to find the probability that at least one outcome of the element will occur. This given by the general formula

P(at least one event occurring) $= 1 - P$(no outcomes occurring). For example, to find the probability that at least one even number will show when a pair of dice is rolled, find the probability that two odd numbers will be rolled (no even numbers) and subtract from one. You can always use a tree diagram or make a chart to list the possible outcomes when the sample space is small, such as in the dice-rolling example, but in most cases it will be much faster to use the multiplication and complement formulas.

Expected value is a method of determining expected outcome in a random situation. It is really a sum of the weighted probabilities of the possible outcomes. Multiply the probability of an event occurring by the weight assigned to that probability (such as the amount of money won or lost). A practical application of the expected value is to determine whether a game of chance is really fair. If the sum of the weighted probabilities is equal to zero, the game is generally considered fair because the player has a fair chance to at least to break even. If the expected value is less than zero, then players lose more than they win. For example, a lottery drawing might allow the player to choose any three-digit number, 000–999. The probability of choosing the winning number is 1:1000. If it costs \$1 to play, and a winning number receives \$500, the expected value is $\left(-\$1 \cdot \frac{999}{1,000}\right) +$ $\left(\$500 \cdot \frac{1}{1,000}\right) = -0.499$ or $-\$0.50$. You can expect to lose on average 50 cents for every dollar you spend.

Most of the time, when we talk about probability, we mean theoretical probability. **Empirical probability**, or experimental probability or relative frequency, is the number of times an outcome occurs in a particular experiment or a certain number of observed events. While theoretical probability is based on what *should* happen, experimental probability is based on what *has* happened. Experimental probability is calculated in the same way as theoretical, except that actual outcomes are used instead of possible outcomes.

Theoretical and experimental probability do not always line up with one another. Theoretical probability says that out of 20 coin tosses, 10 should be heads. However, if we were actually to toss 20 coins, we might record just 5 heads. This doesn't mean that our theoretical probability is incorrect; it just means that this particular experiment had results that were different from what was predicted. A practical application of empirical probability is the insurance industry. There are no set functions that define life span, health, or safety. Insurance companies look at factors from hundreds of thousands of individuals to find patterns that they then use to set the formulas for insurance premiums.

Statistics

Statistics is the branch of mathematics that deals with collecting, recording, interpreting, illustrating, and analyzing large amounts of data. The following terms are often used in the discussion of data and statistics:
Data – the collective name for pieces of information (singular is datum).
Quantitative data – measurements (such as length, mass, and speed) that provide information about quantities in numbers
Qualitative data – information (such as colors, scents, tastes, and shapes) that cannot be measured using numbers
Discrete data – information that can be expressed only by a specific value, such as whole or half numbers; For example, since people can be counted only in whole numbers, a population count would be discrete data.

Continuous data – information (such as time and temperature) that can be expressed by any value within a given range

Primary data – information that has been collected directly from a survey, investigation, or experiment, such as a questionnaire or the recording of daily temperatures; Primary data that has not yet been organized or analyzed is called raw data.

Secondary data – information that has been collected, sorted, and processed by the researcher

Ordinal data – information that can be placed in numerical order, such as age or weight

Nominal data – information that cannot be placed in numerical order, such as names or places

Measures of Central Tendency

The quantities of mean, median, and mode are all referred to as measures of central tendency. They can each give a picture of what the whole set of data looks like with just a single number. Knowing what each of these values represents is vital to making use of the information they provide.

The mean, also known as the arithmetic mean or average, of a data set is calculated by summing all of the values in the set and dividing that sum by the number of values. For example, if a data set has 6 numbers and the sum of those 6 numbers is 30, the mean is calculated as 30/6 = 5.

The median is the middle value of a data set. The median can be found by putting the data set in numerical order, and locating the middle value. In the data set (1, 2, 3, 4, 5), the median is 3. If there is an even number of values in the set, the median is calculated by taking the average of the two middle values. In the data set, (1, 2, 3, 4, 5, 6), the median would be (3 + 4)/2 = 3.5.

The mode is the value that appears most frequently in the data set. In the data set (1, 2, 3, 4, 5, 5, 5), the mode would be 5 since the value 5 appears three times. If multiple values appear the same number of times, there are multiple values for the mode. If the data set were (1, 2, 2, 3, 4, 4, 5, 5), the modes would be 2, 4, and 5. If no value appears more than any other value in the data set, then there is no mode.

Measures of Dispersion

The standard deviation expresses how spread out the values of a distribution are from the mean. Standard deviation is given in the same units as the original data and is represented by a lower case sigma (σ).

A high standard deviation means that the values are very spread out. A low standard deviation means that the values are close together.

If every value in a distribution is increased or decreased by the same amount, the mean, median, and mode are increased or decreased by that amount, but the standard deviation stays the same.

If every value in a distribution is multiplied or divided by the same number, the mean, median, mode, and standard deviation will all be multiplied or divided by that number.

The range of a distribution is the difference between the highest and lowest values in the distribution. For example, in the data set (1, 3, 5, 7, 9, 11), the highest and lowest values are 11 and 1, respectively. The range then would be calculated as 11 – 1 = 10.

The three quartiles are the three values that divide a data set into four equal parts. Quartiles are generally only calculated for data sets with a large number of values. As a simple example, for the data set consisting of the numbers 1 through 99, the first quartile (Q1) would be 25, the second quartile (Q2), always equal to the median, would be 50, and the third quartile (Q3) would be 75. The difference between Q1 and Q3 is known as the interquartile range.

Displaying data

A bar graph is a graph that uses bars to compare data, as if each bar were a ruler being used to measure the data. The graph includes a scale that identifies the units being measured.

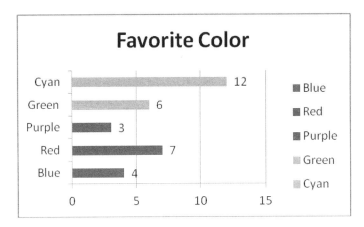

A line graph is a graph that connects points to show how data increases or decreases over time. The time line is the horizontal axis. The connecting lines between data points on the graph are a way to more clearly show how the data changes.

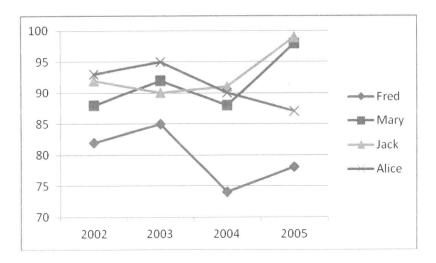

A pictograph is a graph that uses pictures or symbols to show data. The pictograph will have a key to identify what each symbol represents. Generally, each symbol stands for one or more objects.

A pie chart or circle graph is a diagram used to compare parts of a whole. The full pie represents the whole, and it is divided into sectors that each represent something that is a part of the whole. Each sector or slice of the pie is either labeled to indicate what it represents, or explained on a key associated with the chart. The size of each slice is determined by the percentage of the whole that the associated quantity represents. Numerically, the angle measurement of each sector can be computed by solving the proportion: x/360 = part/whole.

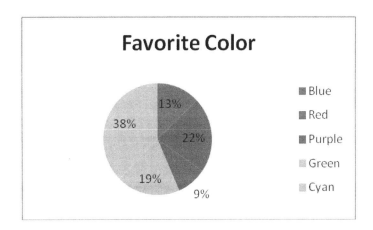

A histogram is a special type of bar graph where the data are grouped in intervals (for example 20-29, 30-39, 40-49, etc.). The frequency, or number of times a value occurs in each interval, is indicated by the height of the bar. The intervals do not have to be the same amount but usually are (all data in ranges of 10 or all in ranges of 5, for example). The smaller the intervals, the more detailed the information.

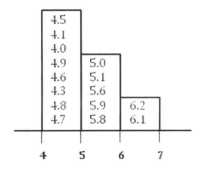

A stem-and-leaf plot is a way to organize data visually so that the information is easy to understand. A stem-and-leaf plot is simple to construct because a simple line separates the stem (the part of the plot listing the tens digit, if displaying two-digit data) from the leaf (the part that shows the ones digit). Thus, the number 45 would appear as 4 | 5. The stem-and-leaf plot for test scores of a group of 11 students might look like the following:

9 | 5
8 | 1, 3, 8
7 | 0, 2, 4, 6, 7
6 | 2, 8

A stem-and-leaf plot is similar to a histogram or other frequency plot, but with a stem-and-leaf plot, all the original data is preserved. In this example, it can be seen at a glance that nearly half the students scored in the 70's, yet all the data has been maintained. These plots can be used for larger numbers as well, but they tend to work better for small sets of data as they can become unwieldy with larger sets.

Natural Sciences

Scientific Method

One could argue that scientific knowledge is the sum of all scientific inquiries for truths about the natural world carried out throughout the history of human kind. More simply put, it is thanks to scientific inquiry that we know what we do about the world. Scientists use a number of generally accepted techniques collectively known as the scientific method. The scientific method generally involves carrying out the following steps:

- Identifying a problem or posing a question
- Formulating a hypothesis or an educated guess
- Conducting experiments or tests that will provide a basis to solve the problem or answer the question
- Observing the results of the test
- Drawing conclusions

An important part of the scientific method is using acceptable experimentation techniques to ensure results are not skewed. Objectivity is also important if valid results are to be obtained. Another important part of the scientific method is peer review. It is essential that experiments be performed and data be recorded in such a way that experiments can be reproduced to verify results.

A scientific fact is considered an objective and verifiable observation. A scientific theory is a greater body of accepted knowledge, principles, or relationships that might explain a fact. A hypothesis is an educated guess that is not yet proven. It is used to predict the outcome of an experiment in an attempt to solve a problem or answer a question. A law is an explanation of events that always lead to the same outcome. It is a fact that an object falls. The law of gravity explains why an object falls. The theory of relativity, although generally accepted, has been neither proven nor disproved. A model is used to explain something on a smaller scale or in simpler terms to provide an example. It is a representation of an idea that can be used to explain events or applied to new situations to predict outcomes or determine results.

History of Science

When one examines the history of scientific knowledge, it is clear that it is constantly evolving. The body of facts, models, theories, and laws grows and changes over time. In other words, one scientific discovery leads to the next. Some advances in science and technology have important and long-lasting effects on science and society. Some discoveries were so alien to the accepted beliefs of the time that not only were they rejected as wrong, but were also considered outright blasphemy. Today, however, many beliefs once considered incorrect have become an ingrained part of scientific knowledge, and have also been the basis of new advances. Examples of advances include: Copernicus's heliocentric view of the universe, Newton's laws of motion and planetary orbits, relativity, geologic time scale, plate tectonics, atomic theory, nuclear physics, biological evolution, germ theory, industrial revolution, molecular biology, information and communication, quantum theory, galactic universe, and medical and health technology.

Anton van Leeuwenhoek (d. 1723) used homemade magnifying glasses to become the first person to observe single-celled organisms. He observed bacteria, yeast, plants, and other microscopic organisms. His observations contributed to the field of microbiology. Carl Linnaeus (d. 1778) created a method to classify plants and animals, which became known as the Linnaean taxonomy. This was an important contribution because it offered a way to organize and therefore study large amounts of data. Charles Robert Darwin (d. 1882) is best known for contributing to the survival of the fittest through natural selection theory of evolution by observing different species of birds, specifically finches, in various geographic locations. Although the species Darwin looked at were different, he speculated they had a common ancestor. He reasoned that specific traits persisted because they gave the birds a greater chance of surviving and reproducing. He also discovered fossils, noted stratification, dissected marine animals, and interacted with indigenous peoples. He contributed to the fields of biology, marine biology, anthropology, paleontology, geography, and zoology.

Gregor Johann Mendel (d. 1884) is famous for experimenting with pea plants to observe the occurrence of inherited traits. He eventually became known as the father of genetics. Barbara McClintock (d. 1992) created the first genetic map for maize and was able to demonstrate basic genetic principles, such as how recombination is an exchange of chromosomal information. She also discovered how transposition flips the switch for traits. Her work contributed to the field of genetics, in particular to areas of study concerned with the structure and function of cells and chromosomes. James Watson and Francis Crick (d. 2004) were co-discoverers of the structure of deoxyribonucleic acid (DNA), which has a double helix shape. DNA contains the code for genetic information. The discovery of the double helix shape was important because it helped to explain how DNA replicates.

Mathematics of Science

Using the metric system is generally accepted as the preferred method for taking measurements. Having a universal standard allows individuals to interpret measurements more easily, regardless of where they are located. The basic units of measurement are: the meter, which measures length; the liter, which measures volume; and the gram, which measures mass. The metric system starts with a base unit and increases or decreases in units of 10. The prefix and the base unit combined are used to indicate an amount. For example, deka is 10 times the base unit. A dekameter is 10 meters; a dekaliter is 10 liters; and a dekagram is 10 grams. The prefix hecto refers to 100 times the base amount; kilo is 1,000 times the base amount. The prefixes that indicate a fraction of the base unit are deci, which is 1/10 of the base unit; centi, which is 1/100 of the base unit; and milli, which is 1/1000 of the base unit.

The mathematical concept of significant figures or significant digits is often used to determine the precision of measurements or the level of confidence one has in a specific measurement. The significant figures of a measurement include all the digits known with certainty plus one estimated or uncertain digit. There are a number of rules for determining which digits are considered "important" or "interesting." They are: all non-zero digits are significant, zeros between digits are significant, and leading and trailing zeros are not significant unless they appear to the right of the non-zero digits in a decimal. For example, in 0.01230 the significant digits are 1230, and this number would be said to be accurate to the hundred-thousandths place. The zero indicates that the amount has actually been measured as 0. Other zeros are considered place holders, and are not important. A decimal point may be placed after zeros to indicate their importance (in 100. for example).

Scientific notation is used because values in science can be very large or very small, which makes them unwieldy. A number in decimal notation is 93,000,000. In scientific notation, it is 9.3×10^7. The first number, 9.3, is the coefficient. It is always greater than or equal to 1 and less than 10. This number is followed by a multiplication sign. The base is always 10 in scientific notation. If the number is greater than ten, the exponent is positive. If the number is between zero and one, the exponent is negative. The first digit of the number is followed by a decimal point and then the rest of the number. In this case, the number is 9.3. To get that number, the decimal point was moved seven places from the end of the number, 93,000,000. The number of places, seven, is the exponent.

Statistics

Data collected during a science lab can be organized and presented in any number of ways. While straight narrative is a suitable method for presenting some lab results, it is not a suitable way to present numbers and quantitative measurements. These types of observations can often be better presented with tables and graphs. Data that is presented in tables and organized in rows and columns may also be used to make graphs quite easily. Other methods of presenting data include illustrations, photographs, video, and even audio formats. In a formal report, tables and figures are labeled and referred to by their labels. For example, a picture of a bubbly solution might be labeled Figure 1, Bubbly Solution. It would be referred to in the text in the following way: "The reaction created bubbles 10 mm in size, as shown in Figure 1, Bubbly Solution." Graphs are also labeled as figures. Tables are labeled in a different way. Examples include: Table 1, Results of Statistical Analysis, or Table 2, Data from Lab 2.

Graphs and charts are effective ways to present scientific data such as observations, statistical analyses, and comparisons between dependent variables and independent variables. On a line chart, the independent variable (the one that is being manipulated for the experiment) is represented on the horizontal axis (the x-axis). Any dependent variables (the ones that may change as the independent variable changes) are represented on the y-axis. The points are charted and a line is drawn to connect the points. An XY or scatter plot is often used to plot many points. A "best fit" line is drawn, which allows outliers to be identified more easily. Charts and their axes should have titles. The x and y interval units should be evenly spaced and labeled. Other types of charts are bar charts and histograms, which can be used to compare differences between the data collected for two variables. A pie chart can graphically show the relation of parts to a whole.

Mean: The mean is the sum of a list of numbers divided by the number of numbers.
Median: The median is the middle number in a list of numbers sorted from least to greatest. If the list has an even number of entries, the median is the smaller of the two in the middle.
Standard deviation: This measures the variability of a data set and determines the amount of confidence one can have in the conclusions.
Mode: This is the value that appears most frequently in a data set.
Range: This is the difference between the highest and lowest numbers, which can be used to determine how spread out data is.
Regression Analysis: This is a method of analyzing sets of data and sets of variables that involves studying how the typical value of the dependent variable changes when any one of the independent variables is varied and the other independent variables remain fixed.

Geology

Minerals are naturally occurring, inorganic solids with a definite chemical composition and an orderly internal crystal structure. A polymorph is two minerals with the same chemical

geology = physical structure

petrology = study of Rocks

mineralogy = study of mineral

composition, but a different crystal structure. Rocks are aggregates of one or more minerals, and may also contain mineraloids (minerals lacking a crystalline structure) and organic remains. The three types of rocks are sedimentary, igneous, and metamorphic. Rocks are classified based on their formation and the minerals they contain. Minerals are classified by their chemical composition. Geology is the study of the planet Earth as it pertains to the composition, structure, and origin of its rocks. Petrology is the study of rocks, including their composition, texture, structure, occurrence, mode of formation, and history. Mineralogy is the study of minerals.

Sedimentary rocks are formed by the process of lithification, which involves compaction, the expulsion of liquids from pores, and the cementation of the pre-existing rock. It is pressure and temperature that are responsible for this process. Sedimentary rocks are often formed in layers in the presence of water, and may contain organic remains, such as fossils. Sedimentary rocks are organized into three groups: detrital, biogenic, and chemical. Texture refers to the size, shape, and grains of sedimentary rock. Texture can be used to determine how a particular sedimentary rock was created. Composition refers to the types of minerals present in the rock. The origin of sedimentary rock refers to the type of water that was involved in its creation. Marine deposits, for example, likely involved ocean environments, while continental deposits likely involved dry land and lakes.

Igneous rock is formed from magma, which is molten material originating from beneath the Earth's surface. Depending upon where magma cools, the resulting igneous rock can be classified as intrusive, plutonic, hypabyssal, extrusive, or volcanic. Magma that solidifies at a depth is intrusive, cools slowly, and has a coarse grain as a result. An example is granite. Magma that solidifies at or near the surface is extrusive, cools quickly, and usually has a fine grain. An example is basalt. Magma that actually flows out of the Earth's surface is called lava. Some extrusive rock cools so quickly that crystals do not have time to form. These rocks have a glassy appearance. An example is obsidian. Hypabyssal rock is igneous rock that is formed at medium depths.

Metamorphic rock is that which has been changed by great heat and pressure. This results in a variety of outcomes, including deformation, compaction, destruction of the characteristics of the original rock, bending, folding, and formation of new minerals because of chemical reactions, and changes in the size and shape of the mineral grain. For example, the igneous rock ferromagnesian can be changed into schist and gneiss. The sedimentary rock carbonaceous can be changed into marble. The texture of metamorphic rocks can be classified as foliated and unfoliated. Foliation, or layering, occurs when rock is compressed along one axis during recrystallization. This can be seen in schist and shale. Unfoliated rock does not include this banding. Rocks that are compressed equally from all sides or lack specific minerals will be unfoliated. An example is marble.

Fossils are preservations of plants, animals, their remains, or their traces that date back to about 10,000 years ago. Fossils and where they are found in rock strata makes up the fossil record. Fossils are formed under a very specific set of conditions. The fossil must not be damaged by predators and scavengers after death, and the fossil must not decompose. Usually, this happens when the organism is quickly covered with sediment. This sediment builds up and molecules in the organism's body are replaced by minerals. Fossils come in an array of sizes, from single-celled organisms to large dinosaurs.

Plate Tectonics

The Earth is ellipsoid, not perfectly spherical. This means the diameter is different through the poles and at the equator. Through the poles, the Earth is about 12,715 km in diameter. The approximate center of the Earth is at a depth of 6,378 km. The Earth is divided into a crust, mantle, and core. The core consists of a solid inner portion. Moving outward, the molten outer core occupies the space from about a depth of 5,150 km to a depth of 2,890 km. The mantle consists of a lower and upper layer. The lower layer includes the D' (D prime) and D" (D double-prime) layers. The solid portion of the upper mantle and crust together form the lithosphere, or rocky sphere. Below this, but still within the mantle, is the asthenosphere, or weak sphere. These layers are distinguishable because the lithosphere is relatively rigid, while the asthenosphere resembles a thick liquid.

The theory of plate tectonics states that the lithosphere, the solid portion of the mantle and Earth's crust, consists of major and minor plates. These plates are on top of and move with the viscous upper mantle, which is heated because of the convection cycle that occurs in the interior of the Earth. There are different estimates as to the exact number of major and minor plates. The number of major plates is believed to be between 9 and 15, and it is thought that there may be as many as 40 minor plates. The United States is atop the North American plate. The Pacific Ocean is atop the Pacific plate. The point at which these two plates slide horizontally along the San Andreas fault is an example of a transform plate boundary. The other two types of boundaries are divergent (plates that are spreading apart and forming new crust) and convergent (the process of subduction causes one plate to go under another). The movement of plates is what causes other features of the Earth's crust, such as mountains, volcanoes, and earthquakes.

Volcanoes can occur along any type of tectonic plate boundary. At a divergent boundary, as plates move apart, magma rises to the surface, cools, and forms a ridge. An example of this is the mid-Atlantic ridge. Convergent boundaries, where one plate slides under another, are often areas with a lot of volcanic activity. The subduction process creates magma. When it rises to the surface, volcanoes can be created. Volcanoes can also be created in the middle of a plate over hot spots. Hot spots are locations where narrow plumes of magma rise through the mantle in a fixed place over a long period of time. The Hawaiian Islands and Midway are examples. The plate shifts and the island moves. Magma continues to rise through the mantle, however, which produces another island. Volcanoes can be active, dormant, or extinct. Active volcanoes are those that are erupting or about to erupt. Dormant volcanoes are those that might erupt in the future and still have internal volcanic activity. Extinct volcanoes are those that will not erupt.

Geography

For the purposes of tracking time and location, the Earth is divided into sections with imaginary lines. Lines that run vertically around the globe through the poles are lines of longitude, sometimes called meridians. The Prime Meridian is the longitudinal reference point of 0. Longitude is measured in 15-degree increments toward the east or west. Degrees are further divided into 60 minutes, and each minute is divided into 60 seconds. Lines of latitude run horizontally around the Earth parallel to the equator, which is the 0 reference point and the widest point of the Earth. Latitude is the distance north or south from the equator, and is also measured in degrees, minutes, and seconds.

Tropic of Cancer: This is located at 23.5 degrees north. The Sun is directly overhead at noon on June 21 in the Tropic of Cancer, which marks the beginning of summer in the Northern Hemisphere. **Tropic of Capricorn**: This is located at 23.5 degrees south. The Sun is directly overhead at noon on December 21 in the Tropic of Capricorn, which marks the beginning of winter in the Northern Hemisphere.
Arctic Circle: This is located at 66.5 degrees north, and marks the start of when the Sun is not

visible above the horizon. This occurs on December 21, the same day the Sun is directly over the Tropic of Capricorn.

Antarctic Circle: This is located at 66.5 degrees south, and marks the start of when the Sun is not visible above the horizon. This occurs on June 21, which marks the beginning of winter in the Southern Hemisphere and is when the Sun is directly over the Tropic of Cancer.

Latitude is a measurement of the distance from the equator. The distance from the equator indicates how much solar radiation a particular area receives. The equator receives more sunlight, while polar areas receive less. The Earth tilts slightly on its rotational axis. This tilt determines the seasons and affects weather. There are eight biomes or ecosystems with particular climates that are associated with latitude. Those in the high latitudes, which get the least sunlight, are tundra and taiga. Those in the mid latitudes are grassland, temperate forest, and chaparral. Those in latitudes closest to the equator are the warmest. The biomes are desert and tropical rain forest. The eighth biome is the ocean, which is unique because it consists of water and spans the entire globe. Insolation refers to incoming solar radiation. Diurnal variations refer to the daily changes in insolation. The greatest insolation occurs at noon.

The tilt of the Earth on its axis is 23.5°. This tilt causes the seasons and affects the temperature because it affects the amount of Sun the area receives. When the Northern or Southern Hemispheres are tilted toward the Sun, the hemisphere tilted toward the sun experiences summer and the other hemisphere experiences winter. This reverses as the Earth revolves around the Sun. Fall and spring occur between the two extremes. The equator gets the same amount of sunlight every day of the year, about 12 hours, and doesn't experience seasons. Both poles have days during the winter when they are tilted away from the Sun and receive no daylight. The opposite effect occurs during the summer. There are 24 hours of daylight and no night. The summer solstice, the day with the most amount of sunlight, occurs on June 21 in the Northern Hemisphere and on December 21 in the Southern Hemisphere. The winter solstice, the day with the least amount of sunlight, occurs on December 21 in the Northern Hemisphere and on June 21 in the Southern Hemisphere.

Weather, Atmosphere, Water Cycle

Meteorology is the study of the atmosphere, particularly as it pertains to forecasting the weather and understanding its processes. Weather is the condition of the atmosphere at any given moment. Most weather occurs in the troposphere. Weather includes changing events such as clouds, storms, and temperature, as well as more extreme events such as tornadoes, hurricanes, and blizzards. Climate refers to the average weather for a particular area over time, typically at least 30 years. Latitude is an indicator of climate. Changes in climate occur over long time periods.

The hydrologic, or water, cycle refers to water movement on, above, and in the Earth. Water can be in any one of its three states during different phases of the cycle. The three states of water are liquid water, frozen ice, and water vapor. Processes involved in the hydrologic cycle include precipitation, canopy interception, snowmelt, runoff, infiltration, subsurface flow, evaporation, sublimation, advection, condensation, and transpiration. Precipitation occurs when condensed water vapor falls to Earth. Examples include rain, fog drip, and various forms of snow, hail, and sleet. Canopy interception occurs when precipitation lands on plant foliage instead of falling to the ground and evaporating. Snowmelt is runoff produced by melting snow. Infiltration occurs when water flows from the surface into the ground. Subsurface flow refers to water that flows underground. Evaporation occurs when water in a liquid state changes to a gas. Sublimation occurs when water in a solid state (such as snow or ice) changes to water vapor without going through a liquid phase.

Advection is the movement of water through the atmosphere. Condensation occurs when water vapor changes to liquid water. Transpiration occurs when water vapor is released from plants into the air.

The ocean is the salty body of water that encompasses the Earth. It has a mass of 1.4×1024 grams. Geographically, the ocean is divided into three large oceans: the Pacific Ocean, the Atlantic Ocean, and the Indian Ocean. There are also other divisions, such as gulfs, bays, and various types of seas, including Mediterranean and marginal seas. Ocean distances can be measured by latitude, longitude, degrees, meters, miles, and nautical miles. The ocean accounts for 70.8% of the surface of the Earth, amounting to 361,254,000 km^2. The ocean's depth is greatest at Challenger Deep in the Mariana Trench. The ocean floor here is 10,924 meters below sea level. The depths of the ocean are mapped by echo sounders and satellite altimeter systems. Echo sounders emit a sound pulse from the surface and record the time it takes to return. Satellite altimeters provide better maps of the ocean floor.

The atmosphere consists of 78% nitrogen, 21% oxygen, and 1% argon. It also includes traces of water vapor, carbon dioxide and other gases, dust particles, and chemicals from Earth. The atmosphere becomes thinner the farther it is from the Earth's surface. It becomes difficult to breathe at about 3 km above sea level. The atmosphere gradually fades into space. The lowest layer of the atmosphere is called the troposphere. Its thickness varies at the poles and the equator, varying from about 7 to 17 km. This is where most weather occurs. The stratosphere is next, and continues to an elevation of about 51 km. The mesosphere extends from the stratosphere to an elevation of about 81 km. It is the coldest layer and is where meteors tend to ablate. The next layer is the thermosphere. It is where the International Space Station orbits. The exosphere is the outermost layer, extends to 10,000 km, and mainly consists of hydrogen and helium.

Earth's atmosphere has five main layers. From lowest to highest, these are the troposphere, the stratosphere, the mesosphere, the thermosphere, and the exosphere. Between each pair of layers is a transition layer called a pause. The troposphere includes the tropopause, which is the transitional layer of the stratosphere. Energy from Earth's surface is transferred to the troposphere. Temperature decreases with altitude in this layer. In the stratosphere, the temperature is inverted, meaning that it increases with altitude. The stratosphere includes the ozone layer, which helps block ultraviolet light from the Sun. The stratopause is the transitional layer to the mesosphere. The temperature of the mesosphere decreases with height. It is considered the coldest place on Earth, and has an average temperature of -85 degrees Celsius. Temperature increases with altitude in the thermosphere, which includes the thermopause. Just past the thermosphere is the exobase, the base layer of the exosphere. Beyond the five main layers are the ionosphere, homosphere, heterosphere, and magnetosphere.

Most clouds can be classified according to the altitude of their base above Earth's surface. High clouds occur at altitudes between 5,000 and 13,000 meters. Middle clouds occur at altitudes between 2,000 and 7,000 meters. Low clouds occur from the Earth's surface to altitudes of 2,000 meters. Types of high clouds include cirrus (Ci), thin wispy mare's tails that consist of ice; cirrocumulus (Cc), small, pillow-like puffs that often appear in rows; and cirrostratus (Cs), thin, sheetlike clouds that often cover the entire sky. Types of middle clouds include altocumulus (Ac), gray-white clouds that consist of liquid water; and altostratus (As), grayish or blue-gray clouds that span the sky. Types of low clouds include stratus (St), gray and fog-like clouds consisting of water droplets that take up the whole sky; stratocumulus (Sc), low-lying, lumpy gray clouds; and nimbostratus (Ns), dark gray clouds with uneven bases that indicate rain or snow. Two types of clouds, cumulus (Cu) and cumulonimbus (Cb), are capable of great vertical growth. They can start at a wide range of altitudes, from the Earth's surface to altitudes of 13,000 meters.

Astronomy

Astronomy is the scientific study of celestial objects and their positions, movements, and structures. Celestial does not refer to the Earth in particular, but does include its motions as it moves through space. Other objects include the Sun, the Moon, planets, satellites, asteroids, meteors, comets, stars, galaxies, the universe, and other space phenomena. The term astronomy has its roots in the Greek words "astro" and "nomos," which means "laws of the stars."

What can be seen of the universe is believed to be at least 93 billion light years across. To put this into perspective, the Milky Way galaxy is about 100,000 light years across. Our view of matter in the universe is that it forms into clumps. Matter is organized into stars, galaxies, clusters of galaxies, superclusters, and the Great Wall of galaxies. Galaxies consist of stars, some with planetary systems. Some estimates state that the universe is about 13 billion years old. It is not considered dense, and is believed to consist of 73 percent dark energy, 23 percent cold dark matter, and 4 percent regular matter. Cosmology is the study of the universe. Interstellar medium (ISM) is the gas and dust in the interstellar space between a galaxy's stars.

The solar system is a planetary system of objects that exist in an ecliptic plane. Objects orbit around and are bound by gravity to a star called the Sun. Objects that orbit around the Sun include: planets, dwarf planets, moons, asteroids, meteoroids, cosmic dust, and comets. The definition of planets has changed. At one time, there were nine planets in the solar system. There are now eight. Planetary objects in the solar system include four inner, terrestrial planets: Mercury, Venus, Earth, and Mars. They are relatively small, dense, rocky, lack rings, and have few or no moons. The four outer, or Jovian, planets are Jupiter, Saturn, Uranus, and Neptune, which are large and have low densities, rings, and moons. They are also known as gas giants. Between the inner and outer planets is the asteroid belt. Beyond Neptune is the Kuiper belt. Within these belts are five dwarf planets: Ceres, Pluto, Haumea, Makemake, and Eris.

The Sun is at the center of the solar system. It is composed of 70% hydrogen (H) and 28% helium (He). The remaining 2% is made up of metals. The Sun is one of 100 billion stars in the Milky Way galaxy. Its diameter is 1,390,000 km, its mass is 1.989×1030 kg, its surface temperature is 5,800 K, and its core temperature is 15,600,000 K. The Sun represents more than 99.8% of the total mass of the solar system. At the core, the temperature is 15.6 million K, the pressure is 250 billion atmospheres, and the density is more than 150 times that of water. The surface is called the photosphere. The chromosphere lies above this, and the corona, which extends millions of kilometers into space, is next. Sunspots are relatively cool regions on the surface with a temperature of 3,800 K. Temperatures in the corona are over 1,000,000 K. Its magnetosphere, or heliosphere, extends far beyond Pluto.

Mercury: Mercury is the closest to the Sun and is also the smallest planet. It orbits the Sun every 88 days, has no satellites or atmosphere, has a Moon-like surface with craters, appears bright, and is dense and rocky with a large iron core.
Venus: Venus is the second planet from the Sun. It orbits the Sun every 225 days, is very bright, and is similar to Earth in size, gravity, and bulk composition. It has a dense atmosphere composed of carbon dioxide and some sulfur. It is covered with reflective clouds made of sulfuric acid and exhibits signs of volcanism. Lightning and thunder have been recorded on Venus's surface.
Earth: Earth is the third planet from the Sun. It orbits the Sun every 365 days. Approximately 71% of its surface is salt-water oceans. The Earth is rocky, has an atmosphere composed mainly of

oxygen and nitrogen, has one moon, and supports millions of species. It contains the only known life in the solar system.

Mars: Mars it the fourth planet from the Sun. It appears reddish due to iron oxide on the surface, has a thin atmosphere, has a rotational period similar to Earth's, and has seasonal cycles. Surface features of Mars include volcanoes, valleys, deserts, and polar ice caps. Mars has impact craters and the tallest mountain, largest canyon, and perhaps the largest impact crater yet discovered.

Jupiter: Jupiter is the fifth planet from the Sun and the largest planet in the solar system. It consists mainly of hydrogen, and 25% of its mass is made up of helium. It has a fast rotation and has clouds in the tropopause composed of ammonia crystals that are arranged into bands sub-divided into lighter-hued zones and darker belts causing storms and turbulence. Jupiter has wind speeds of 100 m/s, a planetary ring, 63 moons, and a Great Red Spot, which is an anticyclonic storm.

Saturn: Saturn is the sixth planet from the Sun and the second largest planet in the solar system. It is composed of hydrogen, some helium, and trace elements. Saturn has a small core of rock and ice, a thick layer of metallic hydrogen, a gaseous outer layer, wind speeds of up to 1,800 km/h, a system of rings, and 61 moons.

Uranus: Uranus is the seventh planet from the Sun. Its atmosphere is composed mainly of hydrogen and helium, and also contains water, ammonia, methane, and traces of hydrocarbons. With a minimum temperature of 49 K, Uranus has the coldest atmosphere. Uranus has a ring system, a magnetosphere, and 13 moons.

Neptune: Neptune is the eighth planet from the Sun and is the planet with the third largest mass. It has 12 moons, an atmosphere similar to Uranus, a Great Dark Spot, and the strongest sustained winds of any planet (wind speeds can be as high as 2,100 km/h). Neptune is cold (about 55 K) and has a fragmented ring system.

The Earth is about 12,765 km (7,934 miles) in diameter. The Moon is about 3,476 km (2,160 mi) in diameter. The distance between the Earth and the Moon is about 384,401 km (238,910 mi). The diameter of the Sun is approximately 1,390,000 km (866,000 mi). The distance from the Earth to the Sun is 149,598,000 km, also known as 1 Astronomical Unit (AU). The star that is nearest to the solar system is Proxima Centauri. It is about 270,000 AU away. Some distant galaxies are so far away that their light takes several billion years to reach the Earth. In other words, people on Earth see them as they looked billions of years ago.

It takes about one month for the Moon to go through all its phases. Waxing refers to the two weeks during which the Moon goes from a new moon to a full moon. About two weeks is spent waning, going from a full moon to a new moon. The lit part of the Moon always faces the Sun. The phases of waxing are: new moon, during which the Moon is not illuminated and rises and sets with the Sun; crescent moon, during which a tiny sliver is lit; first quarter, during which half the Moon is lit and the phase of the Moon is due south on the meridian; gibbous, during which more than half of the Moon is lit and has a shape similar to a football; right side, during which the Moon is lit; and full moon, during which the Moon is fully illuminated, rises at sunset, and sets at sunrise. After a full moon, the Moon is waning. The phases of waning are: gibbous, during which the left side is lit and the Moon rises after sunset and sets after sunrise; third quarter, during which the Moon is half lit and rises at midnight and sets at noon; crescent, during which a tiny sliver is lit; and new moon, during which the Moon is not illuminated and rises and sets with the Sun.

Cells

The main difference between eukaryotic and prokaryotic cells is that eukaryotic cells have a nucleus and prokaryotic cells do not. Eukaryotic cells are considered more complex, while prokaryotic cells are smaller and simpler. Eukaryotic cells have membrane-bound organelles that perform various functions and contribute to the complexity of these types of cells. Prokaryotic cells do not contain membrane-bound organelles. In prokaryotic cells, the genetic material (DNA) is not contained within a membrane-bound nucleus. Instead, it aggregates in the cytoplasm in a nucleoid. In eukaryotic cells, DNA is mostly contained in chromosomes in the nucleus, although there is some DNA in mitochondria and chloroplasts. Prokaryotic cells usually divide by binary fission and are haploid. Eukaryotic cells divide by mitosis and are diploid. Prokaryotic structures include plasmids, ribosomes, cytoplasm, a cytoskeleton, granules of nutritional substances, a plasma membrane, flagella, and a few others. They are single-celled organisms. Bacteria are prokaryotic cells.

The functions of plant and animal cells vary greatly, and the functions of different cells within a single organism can also be vastly different. Animal and plant cells are similar in structure in that they are eukaryotic, which means they contain a nucleus. The nucleus is a round structure that controls the activities of the cell and contains chromosomes. Both types of cells have cell membranes, cytoplasm, vacuoles, and other structures. The main difference between the two is that plant cells have a cell wall made of cellulose that can handle high levels of pressure within the cell, which can occur when liquid enters a plant cell. Plant cells have chloroplasts that are used during the process of photosynthesis, which is the conversion of sunlight into food. Plant cells usually have one large vacuole, whereas animal cells can have many smaller ones. Plant cells have a regular shape, while the shapes of animal cell can vary.

Plant cells can be much larger than animal cells, ranging from 10 to 100 micrometers. Animal cells are 10 to 30 micrometers in size. Plant cells can have much larger vacuoles that occupy a large portion of the cell. They also have cell walls, which are thick barriers consisting of protein and sugars. Animal cells lack cell walls. Chloroplasts in plants that perform photosynthesis absorb sunlight and convert it into energy. Mitochondria produce energy from food in animal cells. Plant and animal cells are both eukaryotic, meaning they contain a nucleus. Both plant and animal cells duplicate genetic material, separate it, and then divide in half to reproduce. Plant cells build a cell plate between the two new cells, while animal cells make a cleavage furrow and pinch in half. Microtubules are components of the cytoskeleton in both plant and animal cells. Microtubule organizing centers (MTOCs) make microtubules in plant cells, while centrioles make microtubules in animal cells.

Photosynthesis is the conversion of sunlight into energy in plant cells, and also occurs in some types of bacteria and protists. Carbon dioxide and water are converted into glucose during photosynthesis, and light is required during this process. Cyanobacteria are thought to be the descendants of the first organisms to use photosynthesis about 3.5 billion years ago. Photosynthesis is a form of cellular respiration. It occurs in chloroplasts that use thylakoids, which are structures in the membrane that contain light reaction chemicals. Chlorophyll is a pigment that absorbs light. During the process, water is used and oxygen is released. The equation for the chemical reaction that occurs during photosynthesis is $6H_2O + 6CO_2 \rightarrow C_6H_{12}O_6 + 6O_2$. During photosynthesis, six molecules of water and six molecules of carbon dioxide react to form one molecule of sugar and six molecules of oxygen.

The term cell cycle refers to the process by which a cell reproduces, which involves cell growth, the duplication of genetic material, and cell division. Complex organisms with many cells use the cell cycle to replace cells as they lose their functionality and wear out. The entire cell cycle in animal cells can take 24 hours. The time required varies among different cell types. Human skin cells, for example, are constantly reproducing. Some other cells only divide infrequently. Once neurons are mature, they do not grow or divide. The two ways that cells can reproduce are through meiosis and mitosis. When cells replicate through mitosis, the "daughter cell" is an exact replica of the parent cell. When cells divide through meiosis, the daughter cells have different genetic coding than the parent cell. Meiosis only happens in specialized reproductive cells called gametes.

Mitosis is the process of cell reproduction in which a eukaryotic cell splits into two separate, but completely identical, cells. This process is divided into a number of different phases.
Interphase: The cell prepares for division by replicating its genetic and cytoplasmic material. Interphase can be further divided into G1, S, and G2.
Prophase: The chromatin thickens into chromosomes and the nuclear membrane begins to disintegrate. Pairs of centrioles move to opposite sides of the cell and spindle fibers begin to form. The mitotic spindle, formed from cytoskeleton parts, moves chromosomes around within the cell.
Metaphase: The spindle moves to the center of the cell and chromosome pairs align along the center of the spindle structure.
Anaphase: The pairs of chromosomes, called sisters, begin to pull apart, and may bend. When they are separated, they are called daughter chromosomes. Grooves appear in the cell membrane.
Telophase: The spindle disintegrates, the nuclear membranes reform, and the chromosomes revert to chromatin. In animal cells, the membrane is pinched. In plant cells, a new cell wall begins to form.
Cytokinesis: This is the physical splitting of the cell (including the cytoplasm) into two cells. Some believe this occurs following telophase. Others say it occurs from anaphase, as the cell begins to furrow, through telophase, when the cell actually splits into two.

Meiosis is another process by which eukaryotic cells reproduce. However, meiosis is used by more complex life forms such as plants and animals and results in four unique cells rather than two identical cells as in mitosis. Meiosis has the same phases as mitosis, but they happen twice. In addition, different events occur during some phases of meiosis than mitosis. The events that occur during the first phase of meiosis are interphase (I), prophase (I), metaphase (I), anaphase (I), telophase (I), and cytokinesis (I). During this first phase of meiosis, chromosomes cross over, genetic material is exchanged, and tetrads of four chromatids are formed. The nuclear membrane dissolves. Homologous pairs of chromatids are separated and travel to different poles. At this point, there has been one cell division resulting in two cells. Each cell goes through a second cell division, which consists of prophase (II), metaphase (II), anaphase (II), telophase (II), and cytokinesis (II). The result is four daughter cells with different sets of chromosomes. The daughter cells are haploid, which means they contain half the genetic material of the parent cell. The second phase of meiosis is similar to the process of mitosis. Meiosis encourages genetic diversity.

Genetics

Chromosomes consist of genes, which are single units of genetic information. Genes are made up of deoxyribonucleic acid (DNA). DNA is a nucleic acid located in the cell nucleus. There is also DNA in the mitochondria. DNA replicates to pass on genetic information. The DNA in almost all cells is the same. It is also involved in the biosynthesis of proteins. The model or structure of DNA is described as a double helix. A helix is a curve, and a double helix is two congruent curves connected by horizontal members. The model can be likened to a spiral staircase. It is right-handed. The British scientist Rosalind Elsie Franklin is credited with taking the x-ray diffraction image in 1952 that was used by Francis Crick and James Watson to formulate the double-helix model of DNA and speculate about its important role in carrying and transferring genetic information.

DNA has a double helix shape, resembles a twisted ladder, and is compact. It consists of nucleotides. Nucleotides consist of a five-carbon sugar (pentose), a phosphate group, and a nitrogenous base. Two bases pair up to form the rungs of the ladder. The "side rails" or backbone consists of the covalently bonded sugar and phosphate. The bases are attached to each other with hydrogen bonds, which are easily dismantled so replication can occur. Each base is attached to a phosphate and to a sugar. There are four types of nitrogenous bases: adenine (A), guanine (G), cytosine (C), and thymine (T). There are about 3 billion bases in human DNA. The bases are mostly the same in everybody, but their order is different. It is the order of these bases that creates diversity in people. Adenine (A) pairs with thymine (T), and cytosine (C) pairs with guanine (G).

A gene is a portion of DNA that identifies how traits are expressed and passed on in an organism. A gene is part of the genetic code. Collectively, all genes form the genotype of an individual. The genotype includes genes that may not be expressed, such as recessive genes. The phenotype is the physical, visual manifestation of genes. It is determined by the basic genetic information and how genes have been affected by their environment. An allele is a variation of a gene. Also known as a trait, it determines the manifestation of a gene. This manifestation results in a specific physical appearance of some facet of an organism, such as eye color or height. For example the genetic information for eye color is a gene. The gene variations responsible for blue, green, brown, or black eyes are called alleles. Locus (pl. loci) refers to the location of a gene or alleles.

Mendel's laws are the law of segregation (the first law) and the law of independent assortment (the second law). The law of segregation states that there are two alleles and that half of the total number of alleles are contributed by each parent organism. The law of independent assortment states that traits are passed on randomly and are not influenced by other traits. The exception to this is linked traits. A Punnett square can illustrate how alleles combine from the contributing genes to form various phenotypes. One set of a parent's genes are put in columns, while the genes from the other parent are placed in rows. The allele combinations are shown in each cell. When two different alleles are present in a pair, the dominant one is expressed. A Punnett square can be used to predict the outcome of crosses.

Gene traits are represented in pairs with an upper case letter for the dominant trait (A) and a lower case letter for the recessive trait (a). Genes occur in pairs (AA, Aa, or aa). There is one gene on each chromosome half supplied by each parent organism. Since half the genetic material is from each parent, the offspring's traits are represented as a combination of these. A dominant trait only requires one gene of a gene pair for it to be expressed in a phenotype, whereas a recessive requires both genes in order to be manifested. For example, if the mother's genotype is Dd and the father's is dd, the possible combinations are Dd and dd. The dominant trait will be manifested if the genotype is DD or Dd. The recessive trait will be manifested if the genotype is dd. Both DD and dd are homozygous pairs. Dd is heterozygous.

Evolution

Scientific evidence supporting the theory of evolution can be found in biogeography, comparative anatomy and embryology, the fossil record, and molecular evidence. Biogeography studies the geographical distribution of animals and plants. Evidence of evolution related to the area of biogeography includes species that are well suited for extreme environments. The fossil record shows that species lived only for a short time period before becoming extinct. The fossil record can also show the succession of plants and animals. Living fossils are existing species that have not changed much morphologically and are very similar to ancient examples in the fossil record. Examples include the horseshoe crab and ginko. Comparative embryology studies how species are similar in the embryonic stage, but become increasingly specialized and diverse as they age. Vestigial organs are those that still exist, but become nonfunctional. Examples include the hind limbs of whales and the wings of birds that can no longer fly, such as ostriches.

The rate of evolution is affected by the variability of a population. Variability increases the likelihood of evolution. Variability in a population can be increased by mutations, immigration, sexual reproduction (as opposed to asexual reproduction), and size. Natural selection, emigration, and smaller populations can lead to decreased variability. Sexual selection affects evolution. If fewer genes are available, it will limit the number of genes passed on to subsequent generations. Some animal mating behaviors are not as successful as others. A male that does not attract a female because of a weak mating call or dull feathers, for example, will not pass on its genes. Mechanical isolation, which refers to sex organs that do not fit together very well, can also decrease successful mating.

Natural selection: This theory developed by Darwin states that traits that help give a species a survival advantage are passed on to subsequent generations. Members of a species that do not have the advantageous trait die before they reproduce. Darwin's four principles are: from generation to generation, there are various individuals within a species; genes determine variations; more individuals are born than survive to maturation; and specific genes enable an organism to better survive.

Gradualism: This can be contrasted with punctuationism. It is an idea that evolution proceeds at a steady pace and does not include sudden developments of new species or features from one generation to the next.

Punctuated Equilibrium: This can be contrasted with gradualism. It is the idea in evolutionary biology that states that evolution involves long time periods of no change (stasis) accompanied by relatively brief periods (hundreds of thousands of years) of rapid change.

Three types of evolution are divergent, convergent, and parallel. Divergent evolution refers to two species that become different over time. This can be caused by one of the species adapting to a different environment. Convergent evolution refers to two species that start out fairly different, but evolve to share many similar traits. Parallel evolution refers to species that are not similar and do not become more or less similar over time. Mechanisms of evolution include descent (the passing on of genetic information), mutation, migration, natural selection, and genetic variation and drift. The biological definition of species refers to a group of individuals that can mate and reproduce. Speciation refers to the evolution of a new biological species. The biological species concept (BSC) basically states that a species is a community of individuals that can reproduce and have a niche in nature.

One theory of how life originated on Earth is that life developed from nonliving materials. The first stage of this transformation happened when abiotic (nonliving) synthesis took place, which is the formation of monomers like amino acids and nucleotides. Next, monomers joined together to create polymers such as proteins and nucleic acids. These polymers are then believed to have formed into protobionts. The last stage was the development of the process of heredity. Supporters of this theory believe that RNA was the first genetic material. Another theory postulates that hereditary systems came about before the origination of nucleic acids. Another theory is that life, or the precursors for it, were transported to Earth from a meteorite or other object from space. There is no real evidence to support this theory.

A number of scientists have made significant contributions to the theory of evolution:
Cuvier (1744-1829): Cuvier was a French naturalist who used the fossil record (paleontology) to compare the anatomies of extinct species and existing species to make conclusions about extinction. He believed in the catastrophism theory more strongly than the theory of evolution.

Lamarck (1769-1832): Lamarck was a French naturalist who believed in the idea of evolution and thought it was a natural occurrence influenced by the environment. He studied medicine and botany. Lamarck put forth a theory of evolution by inheritance of acquired characteristics. He theorized that organisms became more complex by moving up a ladder of progress.

Lyell (1797-1875): Lyell was a British geologist who believed in geographical uniformitarianism, which can be contrasted with catastrophism.

Charles Robert Darwin (1809-1882): Darwin was an English naturalist known for his belief that evolution occurred by natural selection. He believed that species descend from common ancestors.

Alfred Russell Wallace (1823-1913): He was a British naturalist who independently developed a theory of evolution by natural selection. He believed in the transmutation of species (that one species develops into another).

Organism Classification

The groupings in the five kingdom classification system are kingdom, phylum/division, class, order, family, genus, and species. A memory aid for this is: King Phillip Came Over For Good Soup. The five kingdoms are Monera, Protista, Fungi, Plantae, and Animalia. The kingdom is the top level classification in this system. Below that are the following groupings: phylum, class, order, family, genus, and species. The Monera kingdom includes about 10,000 known species of prokaryotes, such as bacteria and cyanobacteria. Members of this kingdom can be unicellular organisms or colonies. The next four kingdoms consist of eukaryotes. The Protista kingdom includes about 250,000 species of unicellular protozoans and unicellular and multicellular algae. The Fungi kingdom includes about 100,000 species. A recently introduced system of classification includes a three domain grouping above kingdom. The domain groupings are Archaea, Bacteria (which both consist of prokaryotes), and Eukarya, which include eukaryotes. According to the five kingdom classification system, humans are: kingdom Animalia, phylum Chordata, subphylum Vertebrata, class Mammalia, order Primate, family Hominidae, genus Homo, and species Sapiens.

An organism is a living thing. A unicellular organism is an organism that has only one cell. Examples of unicellular organisms are bacteria and paramecium. A multicellular organism is one that consists of many cells. Humans are a good example. By some estimates, the human body is made up of billions of cells. Others think the human body has more than 75 trillion cells. The term microbe refers to small organisms that are only visible through a microscope. Examples include viruses, bacteria, fungi, and protozoa. Microbes are also referred to as microorganisms, and it is these that are studied by microbiologists. Bacteria can be rod shaped, round (cocci), or spiral (spirilla). These shapes are used to differentiate among types of bacteria. Bacteria can be identified by staining them. This particular type of stain is called a gram stain. If bacteria are gram-positive, they absorb the stain and become purple. If bacteria are gram-negative, they do not absorb the stain and become a pinkish color.

Organisms in the Protista kingdom are classified according to their methods of locomotion, their methods of reproduction, and how they get their nutrients. Protists can move by the use of a flagellum, cilia, or pseudopod. Flagellates have flagellum, which are long tails or whip-like structures that are rotated to help the protist move. Ciliates use cilia, which are smaller hair-like structures on the exterior of a cell that wiggle to help move the surrounding matter. Amoeboids use pseudopodia to move. Bacteria reproduce either sexually or asexually. Binary fission is a form of asexual reproduction whereby bacteria divide in half to produce two new organisms that are clones of the parent. In sexual reproduction, genetic material is exchanged. When kingdom members are categorized according to how they obtain nutrients, the three types of protists are photosynthetic, consumers, and saprophytes. Photosynthetic protists convert sunlight into energy. Organisms that use photosynthesis are considered producers. Consumers, also known as heterotrophs, eat or consume other organisms. Saprophytes consume dead or decaying substances.

Mycology is the study of fungi. The Fungi kingdom includes about 100,000 species. They are further delineated as mushrooms, yeasts, molds, rusts, mildews, stinkhorns, puffballs, and truffles. Fungi are characterized by cell walls that have chitin, a long chain polymer carbohydrate. Fungi are different from species in the Plant kingdom, which have cell walls consisting of cellulose. Fungi are thought to have evolved from a single ancestor. Although they are often thought of as a type of plant, they are more similar to animals than plants. Fungi are typically small and numerous, and have a diverse morphology among species. They can have bright red cups and be orange jellylike masses, and their shapes can resemble golf balls, bird nests with eggs, starfish, parasols, and male genitalia. Some members of the stinkhorn family emit odors similar to dog scat to attract flies that help transport spores that are involved in reproduction. Fungi of this family are also consumed by humans.

Chlorophyta are green algae. Bryophyta are nonvascular mosses and liverworts. They have root-like parts called rhizoids. Since they do not have the vascular structures to transport water, they live in moist environments. Lycophyta are club mosses. They are vascular plants. They use spores and need water to reproduce. Equisetopsida (sphenophyta) are horsetails. Like lycophyta, they need water to reproduce with spores. They have rhizoids and needle-like leaves. The pteridophytes (filicopsida) are ferns. They have stems (rhizomes). Spermatopsida are the seed plants. Gymnosperms are a conifer, which means they have cones with seeds that are used in reproduction. Plants with seeds require less water. Cycadophyta are cone-bearing and look like palms. Gnetophyta are plants that live in the desert. Coniferophyta are pine trees, and have both cones and needles. Ginkgophyta are ginkos. Anthophyta is the division with the largest number of plant species, and includes flowering plants with true seeds.

Only plants in the division bryophyta (mosses and liverworts) are nonvascular, which means they do not have xylem to transport water. All of the plants in the remaining divisions are vascular, meaning they have true roots, stems, leaves, and xylem. Pteridophytes are plants that use spores and not seeds to reproduce. They include the following divisions: Psilophyta (whisk fern), Lycophyta (club mosses), Sphenophyta (horsetails), and Pterophyta (ferns). Spermatophytes are plants that use seeds to reproduce. Included in this category are gymnosperms, which are flowerless plants that use naked seeds, and angiosperms, which are flowering plants that contain seeds in or on a fruit. Gymnosperms include the following divisions: cycadophyta (cycads), ginkgophyta (maidenhair tree), gnetophyta (ephedra and welwitschia), and coniferophyta (which includes pinophyta conifers). Angiosperms comprise the division anthophyta (flowering plants).

Plants are autotrophs, which mean they make their own food. In a sense, they are self sufficient. Three major processes used by plants are photosynthesis, transpiration, and respiration. Photosynthesis involves using sunlight to make food for plants. Transpiration evaporates water out of plants. Respiration is the utilization of food that was produced during photosynthesis. Two major systems in plants are the shoot and the root system. The shoot system includes leaves, buds, and stems. It also includes the flowers and fruits in flowering plants. The shoot system is located above the ground. The root system is the component of the plant that is underground, and includes roots, tubers, and rhizomes. Meristems form plant cells by mitosis. Cells then differentiate into cell types to form the three types of plant tissues, which are dermal, ground, and vascular. Dermal refers to tissues that form the covering or outer layer of a plant. Ground tissues consist of parenchyma, collenchyma, and/or sclerenchyma cells.

There are at least 230,000 species of flowering plants. They represent about 90 percent of all plants. Angiosperms have a sexual reproduction phase that includes flowering. When growing plants, one may think they develop in the following order: seeds, growth, flowers, and fruit. The reproductive cycle has the following order: flowers, fruit, and seeds. In other words, seeds are the products of successful reproduction. The colors and scents of flowers serve to attract pollinators. Flowers and other plants can also be pollinated by wind. When a pollen grain meets the ovule and is successfully fertilized, the ovule develops into a seed. A seed consists of three parts: the embryo, the endosperm, and a seed coat. The embryo is a small plant that has started to develop, but this development is paused. Germination is when the embryo starts to grow again. The endosperm consists of proteins, carbohydrates, or fats. It typically serves as a food source for the embryo. The seed coat provides protection from disease, insects, and water.

The animal kingdom is comprised of more than one million species in about 30 divisions (the plant kingdom uses the term phyla). There about 800,000 species of insects alone, representing half of all animal species. The characteristics that distinguish members of the animal kingdom from members of other kingdoms are that they are multicellular, are heterotrophic, reproduce sexually (there are some exceptions), have cells that do not contain cell walls or photosynthetic pigments, can move at some stage of life, and can rapidly respond to the environment as a result of specialized tissues like nerve and muscle. Heterotrophic refers to the method of getting energy by eating food that has energy releasing substances. Plants, on the other hand, are autotrophs, which mean they make their own energy. During reproduction, animals have a diploid embryo in the blastula stage. This structure is unique to animals. The blastula resembles a fluid-filled ball.

The animal kingdom includes about one million species. Metazoans are multicellular animals. Food is ingested and enters a mesoderm-lined coelom (body cavity). Phylum porifera and coelenterate are exceptions. The taxonomy of animals involves grouping them into phyla according to body symmetry and plan, as well as the presence of or lack of segmentation. The more complex phyla that have a coelom and a digestive system are further classified as protostomes or deuterostomes according to blastula development. In protostomes, the blastula's blastopore (opening) forms a mouth. In deuterostomes, the blastopore forms an anus. Taxonomy schemes vary, but there are about 36 phyla of animals. The corresponding term for plants at this level is division. The most notable phyla include chordata, mollusca, porifera, cnidaria, platyhelminthes, nematoda, annelida, arthropoda, and echinodermata, which account for about 96 percent of all animal species.

These four animal phyla lack a coelom or have a pseudocoelom.
Porifera: These are sponges. They lack a coelom and get food as water flows through them. They are usually found in marine and sometimes in freshwater environments. They are perforated and diploblastic, meaning there are two layers of cells.
Cnidaria: Members of this phylum are hydrozoa, jellyfish, and obelia. They have radial symmetry, sac-like bodies, and a polyp or medusa (jellyfish) body plan. They are diploblastic, possessing both an ectoderm and an endoderm. Food can get in through a cavity, but members of this phylum do not have an anus.
Platyhelminthes: These are also known as flatworms. Classes include turbellaria (planarian) and trematoda (which include lung, liver, and blood fluke parasites). They have organs and bilateral symmetry. They have three layers of tissue: an ectoderm, a mesoderm, and an endoderm.
Nematoda: These are roundworms. Hookworms and many other parasites are members of this phylum. They have a pseudocoelom, which means the coelom is not completely enclosed within the mesoderm. They also have a digestive tract that runs directly from the mouth to the anus. They are nonsegmented.

Members of the protostomic phyla have mouths that are formed from blastopores.

Mollusca: Classes include bivalvia (organisms with two shells, such as clams, mussels, and oysters), gastropoda (snails and slugs), cephalopoda (octopus, squid, and chambered nautilus), scaphopoda, amphineura (chitons), and monoplacophora.

Annelida: This phylum includes the classes oligochaeta (earthworms), polychaeta (clam worms), and hirudinea (leeches). They have true coeloms enclosed within the mesoderm. They are segmented, have repeating units, and have a nerve trunk.

Arthropoda: The phylum is diverse and populous. Members can be found in all types of environments. They have external skeletons, jointed appendages, bilateral symmetry, and nerve cords. They also have open circulatory systems and sense organs. Subphyla include crustacea (lobster, barnacles, pill bugs, and daphnia), hexapoda (all insects, which have three body segments, six legs, and usual wings), myriapoda (centipedes and millipedes), and chelicerata (the horseshoe crab and arachnids). Pill bugs have gills. Bees, ants, and wasps belong to the order hymenoptera. Like several other insect orders, they undergo complete metamorphosis.

Members of the deuterostomic phyla have anuses that are formed from blastopores.

Echinodermata: Members of this phylum have radial symmetry, are marine organisms, and have a water vascular system. Classes include echinoidea (sea urchins and sand dollars), crinoidea (sea lilies), asteroidea (starfish), ophiuroidea (brittle stars), and holothuroidea (sea cucumbers).

Chordata: This phylum includes humans and all other vertebrates, as well as a few invertebrates (urochordata and cephalochordata). Members of this phylum include agnatha (lampreys and hagfish), gnathostomata, chondrichthyes (cartilaginous fish-like sharks, skates, and rays), osteichthyes (bony fishes, including ray-finned fish that humans eat), amphibians (frogs, salamander, and newts), reptiles (lizards, snakes, crocodiles, and dinosaurs), birds, and mammals.

Anatomy

Extrinsic refers to homeostatic systems that are controlled from outside the body. In higher animals, the nervous system and endocrine system help regulate body functions by responding to stimuli. Hormones in animals regulate many processes, including growth, metabolism, reproduction, and fluid balance. The names of hormones tend to end in "-one." Endocrine hormones are proteins or steroids. Steroid hormones (anabolic steroids) help control the manufacture of protein in muscles and bones.

Invertebrates do not have a backbone, whereas vertebrates do. The great majority of animal species (an estimated 98 percent) are invertebrates, including worms, jellyfish, mollusks, slugs, insects, and spiders. They comprise 30 phyla in all. Vertebrates belong to the phylum chordata. The vertebrate body has two cavities. The thoracic cavity holds the heart and lungs and the abdominal cavity holds the digestive organs. Animals with exoskeletons have skeletons on the outside. Examples are crabs and turtles. Animals with endoskeletons have skeletons on the inside. Examples are humans, tigers, birds, and reptiles.

Major organ systems

Skeletal: This consists of the bones and joints. The skeletal system provides support for the body through its rigid structure, provides protection for internal organs, and works to make organisms motile. Growth hormone affects the rate of reproduction and the size of body cells, and also helps amino acids move through membranes.

Muscular: This includes the muscles. The muscular system allows the body to move and respond to its environment.

Nervous: This includes the brain, spinal cord, and nerves. The nervous system is a signaling system for intrabody communications among systems, responses to stimuli, and interaction within an environment. Signals are electrochemical. Conscious thoughts and memories and sense interpretation occur in the nervous system. It also controls involuntary muscles and functions, such as breathing and the beating of the heart.

Digestive: This includes the mouth, pharynx, esophagus, stomach, intestines, rectum, anal canal, teeth, salivary glands, tongue, liver, gallbladder, pancreas, and appendix. The system helps change food into a form that the body can process and use for energy and nutrients. Food is eventually eliminated as solid waste. Digestive processes can be mechanical, such as chewing food and churning it in the stomach, and chemical, such as secreting hydrochloric acid to kill bacteria and converting protein to amino acids. The overall system converts large food particles into molecules so the body can use them. The small intestine transports the molecules to the circulatory system. The large intestine absorbs nutrients and prepares the unused portions of food for elimination.

Carbohydrates are the primary source of energy as they can be easily converted to glucose. Fats (oils or lipids) are usually not very water soluble, and vitamins A, D, E, and K are fat soluble. Fats are needed to help process these vitamins and can also store energy. Fats have the highest calorie value per gram (9,000 calories). Dietary fiber, or roughage, helps the excretory system. In humans, fiber can help regulate blood sugar levels, reduce heart disease, help food pass through the digestive system, and add bulk. Dietary minerals are chemical elements that are involved with biochemical functions in the body. Proteins consist of amino acids. Proteins are broken down in the body into amino acids that are used for protein biosynthesis or fuel. Vitamins are compounds that are not made by the body, but obtained through the diet. Water is necessary to prevent dehydration since water is lost through the excretory system and perspiration.

Respiratory: This includes the nose, pharynx, larynx, trachea, bronchi, and lungs. It is involved in gas exchange, which occurs in the alveoli. Fish have gills instead of lungs.

Circulatory: This includes the heart, blood, and blood vessels, such as veins, arteries, and capillaries. Blood transports oxygen and nutrients to cells and carbon dioxide to the lungs.

Skin (integumentary): This includes skin, hair, nails, sense receptors, sweat glands, and oil glands. The skin is a sense organ, provides an exterior barrier against disease, regulates body temperature through perspiration, manufactures chemicals and hormones, and provides a place for nerves from the nervous system and parts of the circulation system to travel through. Skin has three layers: epidermis, dermis, and subcutaneous. The epidermis is the thin, outermost, waterproof layer. Basal cells are located in the epidermis. The dermis contains the sweat glands, oil glands, and hair follicles. The subcutaneous layer has connective tissue, and also contains adipose (fat) tissue, nerves, arteries, and veins.

Excretory: This includes the kidneys, ureters, bladder, and urethra. The excretory system helps maintain the amount of fluids in the body. Wastes from the blood system and excess water are removed in urine. The system also helps remove solid waste.

Immune: This includes the lymphatic system, lymph nodes, lymph vessels, thymus, and spleen. Lymph fluid is moved throughout the body by lymph vessels that provide protection against disease. This system protects the body from external intrusions, such as microscopic organisms and foreign substances. It can also protect against some cancerous cells.

Endocrine: This includes the pituitary gland, pineal gland, hypothalamus, thyroid gland, parathyroids, thymus, adrenals, pancreas, ovaries, and testes. It controls systems and processes by secreting hormones into the blood system. Exocrine glands are those that secrete fluid into ducts. Endocrine glands secrete hormones directly into the blood stream without the use of ducts. Prostaglandin (tissue hormones) diffuses only a short distance from the tissue that created it, and influences nearby cells only. Adrenal glands are located above each kidney. The cortex secretes some sex hormones, as well as mineralocorticoids and glucocorticoids involved in immune suppression and stress response. The medulla secretes epinephrine and norepinephrine. Both elevate blood sugar, increase blood pressure, and accelerate heart rate. Epinephrine also stimulates heart muscle. The islets of Langerhans are clumped within the pancreas and secrete glucagon and insulin, thereby regulating blood sugar levels. The four parathyroid glands at the rear of the thyroid secrete parathyroid hormone.

Reproductive: In the male, this system includes the testes, vas deferens, urethra, prostate, penis, and scrotum. In the female, this system includes the ovaries, fallopian tubes (oviduct and uterine tubes), cervix, uterus, vagina, vulva, and mammary glands. Sexual reproduction helps provide genetic diversity as gametes from each parent contribute half the DNA to the zygote offspring. The system provides a method of transporting the male gametes to the female. It also allows for the growth and development of the embryo. Hormones involved are testosterone, interstitial cell stimulating hormone (ICSH), luteinizing hormone (LH), follicle stimulating hormone (FSH), and estrogen. Estrogens secreted from the ovaries include estradiol, estrone, and estriol. They encourage growth, among other things. Progesterone helps prepare the endometrium for pregnancy.

Based on whether or not and when an organism uses meiosis or mitosis, the three possible cycles of reproduction are haplontic, diplontic, and haplodiplontic. Fungi, green algae, and protozoa are haplontic. Animals and some brown algae and fungi are diplontic. Plants and some fungi are haplodiplontic. Diplontic organisms, like multicelled animals, have a dominant diploid life cycle. The haploid generation is simply the egg and sperm. Monoecious species are bisexual (hermaphroditic). In this case, the individual has both male and female organs: sperm-bearing testicles and egg-bearing ovaries. Hermaphroditic species can self fertilize. Some worms are hermaphroditic. Cross fertilization is when individuals exchange genetic information. Most animal species are dioecious, meaning individuals are distinctly male or female.

Biological Relationships

As heterotrophs, animals can be further classified as carnivores, herbivores, omnivores, and parasites. Predation refers to a predator that feeds on another organism, which results in its death. Detritivory refers to heterotrophs that consume organic dead matter. Carnivores are animals that are meat eaters. Herbivores are plant eaters, and omnivores eat both meat and plants. A parasite's food source is its host. A parasite lives off of a host, which does not benefit from the interaction. Nutrients can be classified as carbohydrates, fats, fiber, minerals, proteins, vitamins, and water. Each supply a specific substance required for various species to survive, grow, and reproduce. A calorie is a measurement of heat energy. It can be used to represent both how much energy a food can provide and how much energy an organism needs to live.

Biochemical cycles are how chemical elements required by living organisms cycle between living and nonliving organisms. Elements that are frequently required are phosphorus, sulfur, oxygen, carbon, gaseous nitrogen, and water. Elements can go through gas cycles, sedimentary cycles, or both. Elements circulate through the air in a gas cycle and from land to water in a sedimentary one.

A food chain is a linking of organisms in a community that is based on how they use each other as food sources. Each link in the chain consumes the link above it and is consumed by the link below it. The exceptions are the organism at the top of the food chain and the organism at the bottom. Biomagnification (bioamplification): This refers to an increase in concentration of a substance within a food chain. Examples are pesticides or mercury. Mercury is emitted from coal-fired power plants and gets into the water supply, where it is eaten by a fish. A larger fish eats smaller fish, and humans eat fish. The concentration of mercury in humans has now risen. Biomagnification is affected by the persistence of a chemical, whether it can be broken down and negated, food chain energetics, and whether organisms can reduce or negate the substance.

A food web consists of interconnected food chains in a community. The organisms can be linked to show the direction of energy flow. Energy flow in this sense is used to refer to the actual caloric flow through a system from trophic level to trophic level. Trophic level refers to a link in a food chain or a level of nutrition. The 10% rule is that from trophic level to level, about 90% of the energy is lost (in the form of heat, for example). The lowest trophic level consists of primary producers (usually plants), then primary consumers, then secondary consumers, and finally tertiary consumers (large carnivores). The final link is decomposers, which break down the consumers at the top. Food chains usually do not contain more than six links. These links may also be referred to as ecological pyramids.

Ecosystem stability is a concept that states that a stable ecosystem is perfectly efficient. Seasonal changes or expected climate fluctuations are balanced by homeostasis. It also states that interspecies interactions are part of the balance of the system. Four principles of ecosystem stability are that waste disposal and nutrient replenishment by recycling is complete, the system uses sunlight as an energy source, biodiversity remains, and populations are stable in that they do not over consume resources. Ecologic succession is the concept that states that there is an orderly progression of change within a community. An example of primary succession is that over hundreds of years bare rock decomposes to sand, which eventually leads to soil formation, which eventually leads to the growth of grasses and trees. Secondary succession occurs after a disturbance or major event that greatly affects a community, such as a wild fire or construction of a dam.

Population is a measure of how many individuals exist in a specific area. It can be used to measure the size of human, plant, or animal groups. Population growth depends on many factors. Factors that can limit the number of individuals in a population include lack of resources such as food and water, space, habitat destruction, competition, disease, and predators. Exponential growth refers to an unlimited rising growth rate. This kind of growth can be plotted on a chart in the shape of a J. Carrying capacity is the population size that can be sustained. The world's population is about 6.8 billion and growing. The human population has not yet reached its carrying capacity. Population dynamics refers to how a population changes over time and the factors that cause changes. An S-shaped curve shows that population growth has leveled off. Biotic potential refers to the maximum reproductive capacity of a population given ideal environmental conditions.

Biological concepts

Territoriality: This refers to members of a species protecting areas from other members of their species and from other species. Species members claim specific areas as their own.

Dominance: This refers to the species in a community that is the most populous.

Altruism: This is when a species or individual in a community exhibits behaviors that benefit another individual at a cost to itself. In biology, altruism does not have to be a conscious sacrifice.

Threat display: This refers to behavior by an organism that is intended to intimidate or frighten away members of its own or another species.

The principle of **competitive exclusion** (Gause's Law) states that if there are limited or insufficient resources and species are competing for them, these species will not be able to co-exist. The result is that one of the species will become extinct or be forced to undergo a behavioral or evolutionary change. Another way to say this is that "complete competitors cannot coexist."

A **community** is any number of species interacting within a given area. A **niche** is the role of a species within a community. **Species diversity** refers to the number of species within a community and their populations. A **biome** refers to an area in which species are associated because of climate. The six major biomes in North America are desert, tropical rain forest, grassland, coniferous forest, deciduous forest, and tundra.

Biotic: Biotic factors are the living factors, such as other organisms, that affect a community or population. Abiotic factors are nonliving factors that affect a community or population, such as facets of the environment.

Ecology: Ecology is the study of plants, animals, their environments, and how they interact.

Ecosystem: An ecosystem is a community of species and all of the environment factors that affect them.

Biomass: In ecology, biomass refers to the mass of one or all of the species (species biomass) in an ecosystem or area.

Predation, parasitism, commensalism, and mutualism are all types of species interactions that affect species populations. **Intraspecific relationships** are relationships among members of a species. **Interspecific relationships** are relationships between members of different species.

Predation: This is a relationship in which one individual feeds on another (the prey), causing the prey to die. **Mimicry** is an adaptation developed as a response to predation. It refers to an organism that has a similar appearance to another species, which is meant to fool the predator into thinking the organism is more dangerous than it really is. Two examples are the drone fly and the io moth. The fly looks like a bee, but cannot sting. The io moth has markings on its wings that make it look like an owl. The moth can startle predators and gain time to escape. Predators can also use mimicry to lure their prey.

Commensalism: This refers to interspecific relationships in which one of the organisms benefits. Mutualism, competition, and parasitism are all types of commensalism.
Mutualism: This is a relationship in which both organisms benefit from an interaction.
Competition: This is a relationship in which both organisms are harmed.
Parasitism: This is a relationship in which one organism benefits and the other is harmed.

Atoms

Matter refers to substances that have mass and occupy space (or volume). The traditional definition of matter describes it as having three states: solid, liquid, and gas. These different states are caused by differences in the distances and angles between molecules or atoms, which result in differences in the energy that binds them. Solid structures are rigid or nearly rigid and have strong bonds. Molecules or atoms of liquids move around and have weak bonds, although they are not weak enough to readily break. Molecules or atoms of gases move almost independently of each other, are typically far apart, and do not form bonds. The current definition of matter describes it as having four states. The fourth is plasma, which is an ionized gas that has some electrons that are described as free because they are not bound to an atom or molecule.

All matter consists of atoms. Atoms consist of a nucleus and electrons. The nucleus consists of protons and neutrons. The properties of these are measurable; they have mass and an electrical charge. The nucleus is positively charged due to the presence of protons. Electrons are negatively charged and orbit the nucleus. The nucleus has considerably more mass than the surrounding electrons. Atoms can bond together to make molecules. Atoms that have an equal number of protons and electrons are electrically neutral. If the number of protons and electrons in an atom is not equal, the atom has a positive or negative charge and is an ion.

An element is matter with one particular type of atom. It can be identified by its atomic number, or the number of protons in its nucleus. There are approximately 117 elements currently known, 94 of which occur naturally on Earth. Elements from the periodic table include hydrogen, carbon, iron, helium, mercury, and oxygen. Atoms combine to form molecules. For example, two atoms of hydrogen (H) and one atom of oxygen (O) combine to form water (H_2O).

Compounds are substances containing two or more elements. Compounds are formed by chemical reactions and frequently have different properties than the original elements. Compounds are decomposed by a chemical reaction rather than separated by a physical one.

A solution is a homogeneous mixture. A mixture is two or more different substances that are mixed together, but not combined chemically. Homogeneous mixtures are those that are uniform in their composition. Solutions consist of a solute (the substance that is dissolved) and a solvent (the substance that does the dissolving). An example is sugar water. The solvent is the water and the solute is the sugar. The intermolecular attraction between the solvent and the solute is called solvation. Hydration refers to solutions in which water is the solvent. Solutions are formed when the forces of the molecules of the solute and the solvent are as strong as the individual molecular forces of the solute and the solvent. An example is that salt (NaCl) dissolves in water to create a solution. The Na^+ and the Cl^- ions in salt interact with the molecules of water and vice versa to overcome the individual molecular forces of the solute and the solvent.

Elements are represented in upper case letters. If there is no subscript, it indicates there is only one atom of the element. Otherwise, the subscript indicates the number of atoms. In molecular formulas, elements are organized according to the Hill system. Carbon is first, hydrogen comes next, and the remaining elements are listed in alphabetical order. If there is no carbon, all elements are listed alphabetically. There are a couple of exceptions to these rules. First, oxygen is usually listed last in oxides. Second, in ionic compounds the positive ion is listed first, followed by the negative ion. In CO_2, for example, C indicates 1 atom of carbon and O_2 indicates 2 atoms of oxygen. The compound is carbon dioxide. The formula for ammonia (an ionic compound) is NH_3, which is one atom of nitrogen and three of hydrogen. H_2O is two atoms of hydrogen and one of oxygen. Sugar is $C_6H_{12}O_6$, which is 6 atoms of carbon, 12 of hydrogen, and 6 of oxygen.

An **atom** is one of the most basic units of matter. An atom consists of a central nucleus surrounded by electrons. The **nucleus** of an atom consists of protons and neutrons. It is positively charged, dense, and heavier than the surrounding electrons. The plural form of nucleus is nuclei. **Neutrons** are the uncharged atomic particles contained within the nucleus. The number of neutrons in a nucleus can be represented as "N." Along with neutrons, **protons** make up the nucleus of an atom. The number of protons in the nucleus determines the atomic number of an element. Carbon atoms, for example, have six protons. The atomic number of carbon is 6. **Nucleon** refers collectively to neutrons and protons. **Electrons** are atomic particles that are negatively charged and orbit the nucleus of an atom. The number of protons minus the number of electrons indicates the charge of an atom.

The **atomic number** of an element refers to the number of protons in the nucleus of an atom. It is a unique identifier. It can be represented as Z. Atoms with a neutral charge have an atomic number that is equal to the number of electrons. **Atomic mass** is also known as the mass number. The atomic mass is the total number of protons and neutrons in the nucleus of an atom. It is referred to as "A." The atomic mass (A) is equal to the number of protons (Z) plus the number of neutrons (N). This can be represented by the equation $A = Z + N$. The mass of electrons in an atom is basically insignificant because it is so small. **Atomic weight** may sometimes be referred to as "relative atomic mass," but should not be confused with atomic mass. Atomic weight is the ratio of the average mass per atom of a sample (which can include various isotopes of an element) to 1/12 of the mass of an atom of carbon-12.

Chemical properties are qualities of a substance which can't be determined by simply looking at the substance and must be determined through chemical reactions. Some chemical properties of elements include: atomic number, electron configuration, electrons per shell, electronegativity, atomic radius, and isotopes.

In contrast to chemical properties, **physical properties** can be observed or measured without chemical reactions. These include properties such as color, elasticity, mass, volume, and temperature. **Mass** is a measure of the amount of substance in an object. **Weight** is a measure of the gravitational pull of Earth on an object. **Volume** is a measure of the amount of space occupied. There are many formulas to determine volume. For example, the volume of a cube is the length of one side cubed (a^3) and the volume of a rectangular prism is length times width times height ($l \cdot w \cdot h$). The volume of an irregular shape can be determined by how much water it displaces. **Density** is a measure of the amount of mass per unit volume. The formula to find density is mass divided by volume ($D=m/V$). It is expressed in terms of mass per cubic unit, such as grams per cubic centimeter (g/cm^3). **Specific gravity** is a measure of the ratio of a substance's density compared to the density of water.

Both physical changes and chemical reactions are everyday occurrences. Physical changes do not result in different substances. For example, when water becomes ice it has undergone a physical change, but not a chemical change. It has changed its form, but not its composition. It is still H_2O. Chemical properties are concerned with the constituent particles that make up the physicality of a substance. Chemical properties are apparent when chemical changes occur. The chemical properties of a substance are influenced by its electron configuration, which is determined in part by the number of protons in the nucleus (the atomic number). Carbon, for example, has 6 protons and 6 electrons. It is an element's outermost valence electrons that mainly determine its chemical properties. Chemical reactions may release or consume energy.

Periodic Table

The periodic table groups elements with similar chemical properties together. The grouping of elements is based on atomic structure. It shows periodic trends of physical and chemical properties and identifies families of elements with similar properties. It is a common model for organizing and understanding elements. In the periodic table, each element has its own cell that includes varying amounts of information presented in symbol form about the properties of the element. Cells in the table are arranged in rows (periods) and columns (groups or families). At minimum, a cell includes the symbol for the element and its atomic number. The cell for hydrogen, for example, which appears first in the upper left corner, includes an "H" and a "1" above the letter. Elements are ordered by atomic number, left to right, top to bottom.

In the periodic table, the groups are the columns numbered 1 through 18 that group elements with similar outer electron shell configurations. Since the configuration of the outer electron shell is one of the primary factors affecting an element's chemical properties, elements within the same group have similar chemical properties. Previous naming conventions for groups have included the use of Roman numerals and upper-case letters. Currently, the periodic table groups are: Group 1, alkali metals; Group 2, alkaline earth metals; Groups 3-12, transition metals; Group 13, boron family; Group 14; carbon family; Group 15, pnictogens; Group 16, chalcogens; Group 17, halogens; Group 18, noble gases.

In the periodic table, there are seven periods (rows), and within each period there are blocks that group elements with the same outer electron subshell (more on this in the next section). The number of electrons in that outer shell determines which group an element belongs to within a given block. Each row's number (1, 2, 3, etc.) corresponds to the highest number electron shell that is in use. For example, row 2 uses only electron shells 1 and 2, while row 7 uses all shells from 1-7.

Atomic radii will decrease from left to right across a period (row) on the periodic table. In a group (column), there is an increase in the atomic radii of elements from top to bottom. Ionic radii will be smaller than the atomic radii for metals, but the opposite is true for non-metals. From left to right, electronegativity, or an atom's likeliness of taking another atom's electrons, increases. In a group, electronegativity decreases from top to bottom. Ionization energy or the amount of energy needed to get rid of an atom's outermost electron, increases across a period and decreases down a group. Electron affinity will become more negative across a period but will not change much within a group. The melting point decreases from top to bottom in the metal groups and increases from top to bottom in the non-metal groups.

Electrons

Electrons are subatomic particles that orbit the nucleus at various levels commonly referred to as layers, shells, or clouds. The orbiting electron or electrons account for only a fraction of the atom's mass. They are much smaller than the nucleus, are negatively charged, and exhibit wave-like characteristics. Electrons are part of the lepton family of elementary particles. Electrons can occupy orbits that are varying distances away from the nucleus, and tend to occupy the lowest energy level they can. If an atom has all its electrons in the lowest available positions, it has a stable electron arrangement. The outermost electron shell of an atom in its uncombined state is known as the valence shell. The electrons there are called valence electrons, and it is their number that determines bonding behavior. Atoms tend to react in a manner that will allow them to fill or empty their valence shells.

There are seven electron shells. One is closest to the nucleus and seven is the farthest away. Electron shells can also be identified with the letters K, L, M, N, O, P, and Q. Traditionally, there were four subshells identified by the first letter of their descriptive name: s (sharp), p (principal), d (diffuse), and f (fundamental). The maximum number of electrons for each subshell is as follows: s is 2, p is 6, d is 10, and f is 14. Every shell has an s subshell, the second shell and those above also have a p subshell, the third shell and those above also have a d subshell, and so on. Each subshell contains atomic orbitals, which describes the wave-like characteristics of an electron or a pair of electrons expressed as two angles and the distance from the nucleus. Atomic orbital is a concept used to express the likelihood of an electron's position in accordance with the idea of wave-particle duality.

Electron configuration: This is a trend whereby electrons fill shells and subshells in an element in a particular order and with a particular number of electrons. The chemical properties of the elements reflect their electron configurations. Energy levels (shells) do not have to be completely filled before the next one begins to be filled. An example of electron configuration notation is $1s^2 2s^2 2p^5$, where the first number is the row (period), or shell. The letter refers to the subshell of the shell, and the number in superscript is the number of electrons in the subshell. A common shorthand method for electron configuration notation is to use a noble gas (in a bracket) to abbreviate the shells that elements have in common. For example, the electron configuration for neon is $1s^2 2s^2 2p^6$. The configuration for phosphorus is $1s^2 2s^2 2p^6 3s^2 3p^3$, which can be written as $[Ne]3s^2 3p^3$. Subshells are filled in the following manner: 1s, 2s, 2p, 3s, 3p, 4s, 3d, 4p, 5s, 4d, 5p, 6s, 4f, 5d, 6p, 7s, 5f, 6d, and 7p.

Most atoms are neutral since the positive charge of the protons in the nucleus is balanced by the negative charge of the surrounding electrons. Electrons are transferred between atoms when they come into contact with each other. This creates a molecule or atom in which the number of electrons does not equal the number of protons, which gives it a positive or negative charge. A negative ion is created when an atom gains electrons, while a positive ion is created when an atom loses electrons. An ionic bond is formed between ions with opposite charges. The resulting compound is neutral. Ionization refers to the process by which neutral particles are ionized into charged particles. Gases and plasmas can be partially or fully ionized through ionization.

Atoms interact by transferring or sharing the electrons furthest from the nucleus. Known as the outer or valence electrons, they are responsible for the chemical properties of an element. Bonds between atoms are created when electrons are paired up by being transferred or shared. If electrons are transferred from one atom to another, the bond is ionic. If electrons are shared, the bond is covalent. Atoms of the same element may bond together to form molecules or crystalline solids. When two or more different types of atoms bind together chemically, a compound is made. The physical properties of compounds reflect the nature of the interactions among their molecules. These interactions are determined by the structure of the molecule, including the atoms they consist of and the distances and angles between them.

Isotopes and Molecules

The number of protons in an atom determines the element of that atom. For instance, all helium atoms have exactly two protons, and all oxygen atoms have exactly eight protons. If two atoms have the same number of protons, then they are the same element. However, the number of neutrons in two atoms can be different without the atoms being different elements. Isotope is the term used to distinguish between atoms that have the same number of protons but a different number of neutrons. The names of isotopes have the element name with the mass number. Recall that the mass number is the number of protons plus the number of neutrons. For example, carbon-12 refers to an atom that has 6 protons, which makes it carbon, and 6 neutrons. In other words, 6 protons + 6 neutrons = 12. Carbon-13 has six protons and seven neutrons, and carbon-14 has six protons and eight neutrons. Isotopes can also be written with the mass number in superscript before the element symbol. For example, carbon-12 can be written as ^{12}C.

The important properties of water (H_2O) are high polarity, hydrogen bonding, cohesiveness, adhesiveness, high specific heat, high latent heat, and high heat of vaporization. It is essential to life as we know it, as water is one of the main if not the main constituent of many living things. Water is a liquid at room temperature. The high specific heat of water means it resists the breaking of its hydrogen bonds and resists heat and motion, which is why it has a relatively high boiling point and high vaporization point. It also resists temperature change. Water is peculiar in that its solid state floats in its liquid state. Most substances are denser in their solid forms. Water is cohesive, which means it is attracted to itself. It is also adhesive, which means it readily attracts other molecules. If water tends to adhere to another substance, the substance is said to be hydrophilic. Water makes a good solvent. Substances, particularly those with polar ions and molecules, readily dissolve in water.

Electrons in an atom can orbit different levels around the nucleus. They can absorb or release energy, which can change the location of their orbit or even allow them to break free from the atom. The outermost layer is the valence layer, which contains the valence electrons. The valence layer tends to have or share eight electrons. Molecules are formed by a chemical bond between atoms, a bond which occurs at the valence level. Two basic types of bonds are covalent and ionic. A covalent bond is formed when atoms share electrons. An ionic bond is formed when an atom transfers an electron to another atom. A hydrogen bond is a weak bond between a hydrogen atom of one molecule and an electronegative atom (such as nitrogen, oxygen, or fluorine) of another molecule. The Van der Waals force is a weak force between molecules. This type of force is much weaker than actual chemical bonds between atoms.

Reactions

Chemical reactions measured in human time can take place quickly or slowly. They can take fractions of a second or billions of years. The rates of chemical reactions are determined by how frequently reacting atoms and molecules interact. Rates are also influenced by the temperature and various properties (such as shape) of the reacting materials. Catalysts accelerate chemical reactions, while inhibitors decrease reaction rates. Some types of reactions release energy in the form of heat and light. Some types of reactions involve the transfer of either electrons or hydrogen ions between reacting ions, molecules, or atoms. In other reactions, chemical bonds are broken down by heat or light to form reactive radicals with electrons that will readily form new bonds. Processes such as the formation of ozone and greenhouse gases in the atmosphere and the burning and processing of fossil fuels are controlled by radical reactions.

Chemical equations describe chemical reactions. The reactants are on the left side before the arrow and the products are on the right side after the arrow. The arrow indicates the reaction or change. The coefficient, or stoichiometric coefficient, is the number before the element, and indicates the ratio of reactants to products in terms of moles. The equation for the formation of water from hydrogen and oxygen, for example, is $2H_2(g) + O_2(g) \rightarrow 2H_2O(l)$. The 2 preceding hydrogen and water is the coefficient, which means there are 2 moles of hydrogen and 2 of water. There is 1 mole of oxygen, which does not have to be indicated with the number 1. In parentheses, g stands for gas, l stands for liquid, s stands for solid, and aq stands for aqueous solution (a substance dissolved in water). Charges are shown in superscript for individual ions, but not for ionic compounds. Polyatomic ions are separated by parentheses so the ion will not be confused with the number of ions.

An unbalanced equation is one that does not follow the law of conservation of mass, which states that matter can only be changed, not created. If an equation is unbalanced, the numbers of atoms indicated by the stoichiometric coefficients on each side of the arrow will not be equal. Start by writing the formulas for each species in the reaction. Count the atoms on each side and determine if the number is equal. Coefficients must be whole numbers. Fractional amounts, such as half a molecule, are not possible. Equations can be balanced by multiplying the coefficients by a constant that will produce the smallest possible whole number coefficient. $H_2 + O_2 \rightarrow H_2O$ is an example of an unbalanced equation. The balanced equation is $2H_2 + O_2 \rightarrow 2H_2O$, which indicates that it takes two moles of hydrogen and one of oxygen to produce two moles of water.

One way to organize chemical reactions is to sort them into two categories: oxidation/reduction reactions (also called redox reactions) and metathesis reactions (which include acid/base reactions). Oxidation/reduction reactions can involve the transfer of one or more electrons, or they can occur as a result of the transfer of oxygen, hydrogen, or halogen atoms. The species that loses electrons is oxidized and is referred to as the reducing agent. The species that gains electrons is reduced and is referred to as the oxidizing agent. The element undergoing oxidation experiences an increase in its oxidation number, while the element undergoing reduction experiences a decrease in its oxidation number. Single replacement reactions are types of oxidation/reduction reactions. In a single replacement reaction, electrons are transferred from one chemical species to another. The transfer of electrons results in changes in the nature and charge of the species.

Single substitution, displacement, or replacement reactions are when one reactant is displaced by another to form the final product ($A + BC \rightarrow AB + C$). Single substitution reactions can be cationic or anionic. When a piece of copper (Cu) is placed into a solution of silver nitrate ($AgNO_3$), the solution turns blue. The copper appears to be replaced with a silvery-white material. The equation is $2AgNO_3 + Cu \rightarrow Cu (NO_3)2 + 2Ag$. When this reaction takes place, the copper dissolves and the silver in the silver nitrate solution precipitates (becomes a solid), thus resulting in copper nitrate and silver. Copper and silver have switched places in the nitrate.

Combination, or synthesis, reactions: In a combination reaction, two or more reactants combine to form a single product ($A + B \rightarrow C$). These reactions are also called synthesis or addition reactions. An example is burning hydrogen in air to produce water. The equation is $2H_2 (g) + O_2 (g) \rightarrow 2H_2O (l)$. Another example is when water and sulfur trioxide react to form sulfuric acid. The equation is $H_2O + SO_3 \rightarrow H_2SO_4$.

Double displacement, double replacement, substitution, metathesis, or ion exchange reactions are when ions or bonds are exchanged by two compounds to form different compounds ($AC + BD \rightarrow AD + BC$). An example of this is that silver nitrate and sodium chloride form two different products (silver chloride and sodium nitrate) when they react. The formula for this reaction is $AgNO_3 + NaCl \rightarrow AgCl + NaNO_3$.

Double replacement reactions are metathesis reactions. In a double replacement reaction, the chemical reactants exchange ions but the oxidation state stays the same. One of the indicators of this is the formation of a solid precipitate. In acid/base reactions, an acid is a compound that can donate a proton, while a base is a compound that can accept a proton. In these types of reactions, the acid and base react to form a salt and water. When the proton is donated, the base becomes water and the remaining ions form a salt. One method of determining whether a reaction is an oxidation/reduction or a metathesis reaction is that the oxidation number of atoms does not change during a metathesis reaction.

A neutralization, acid-base, or proton transfer reaction is when one compound acquires H^+ from another. These types of reactions are also usually double displacement reactions. The acid has an H^+ that is transferred to the base and neutralized to form a salt.

Decomposition (or desynthesis, decombination, or deconstruction) reactions; in a decomposition reaction, a reactant is broken down into two or more products ($A \rightarrow B + C$). These reactions are also called analysis reactions. Thermal decomposition is caused by heat. Electrolytic decomposition is due to electricity. An example of this type of reaction is the decomposition of water into hydrogen and oxygen gas. The equation is $2H_2O \rightarrow 2H_2 + O_2$. Decomposition is considered a chemical reaction whereby a single compound breaks down into component parts or simpler compounds. When a compound or substance separates into these simpler substances, the byproducts are often substances that are different from the original. Decomposition can be viewed as the opposite of combination reactions. Most decomposition reactions are endothermic. Heat needs to be added for the chemical reaction to occur. Separation processes can be mechanical or chemical, and usually involve re-organizing a mixture of substances without changing their chemical nature. The separated products may differ from the original mixture in terms of chemical or physical properties. Types of separation processes include filtration, crystallization, distillation, and chromatography. Basically, decomposition breaks down one compound into two or more compounds or substances that are different from the original; separation sorts the substances from the original mixture into like substances.

Endothermic reactions are chemical reactions that absorb heat and exothermic reactions are chemical reactions that release heat. Reactants are the substances that are consumed during a reaction, while products are the substances that are produced or formed. A balanced equation is one that uses reactants, products, and coefficients in such a way that the number of each type of atom (law of conservation of mass) and the total charge remains the same. The reactants are on the left side of the arrow and the products are on the right. The heat difference between endothermic and exothermic reactions is caused by bonds forming and breaking. If more energy is needed to break the reactant bonds than is released when they form, the reaction is endothermic. Heat is absorbed and the environmental temperature decreases. If more energy is released when product bonds form than is needed to break the reactant bonds, the reaction is exothermic. Heat is released and the environmental temperature increases.

The collision theory states that for a chemical reaction to occur, atoms or molecules have to collide with each other with a certain amount of energy. A certain amount of energy is required to breach the activation barrier. Heating a mixture will raise the energy levels of the molecules and the rate of reaction (the time it takes for a reaction to complete). Generally, the rate of reaction is doubled for every 10 degrees Celsius temperature increase. However, the increase needed to double a reaction rate increases as the temperature climbs. This is due to the increase in collision frequency that occurs as the temperature increases. Other factors that can affect the rate of reaction are surface area, concentration, pressure, and the presence of a catalyst.

The particles of an atom's nucleus (the protons and neutrons) are bound together by nuclear force, also known as residual strong force. Unlike chemical reactions, which involve electrons, nuclear reactions occur when two nuclei or nuclear particles collide. This results in the release or absorption of energy and products that are different from the initial particles. The energy released in a nuclear reaction can take various forms, including the release of kinetic energy of the product particles and the emission of very high energy photons known as gamma rays. Some energy may also remain in the nucleus. Radioactivity refers to the particles emitted from nuclei as a result of nuclear instability. There are many nuclear isotopes that are unstable and can spontaneously emit some kind of radiation. The most common types of radiation are alpha, beta, and gamma radiation, but there are several other varieties of radioactive decay.

Inorganic and Organic

The terms inorganic and organic have become less useful over time as their definitions have changed. Historically, inorganic molecules were defined as those of a mineral nature that were not created by biological processes. Organic molecules were defined as those that were produced biologically by a "life process" or "vital force." It was then discovered that organic compounds could be synthesized without a life process. Currently, molecules containing carbon are considered organic. Carbon is largely responsible for creating biological diversity, and is more capable than all other elements of forming large, complex, and diverse molecules of an organic nature. Carbon often completes its valence shell by sharing electrons with other atoms in four covalent bonds, which is also known as tetravalence.

The main trait of inorganic compounds is that they lack carbon. Inorganic compounds include mineral salts, metals and alloys, non-metallic compounds such as phosphorus, and metal complexes. A metal complex has a central atom (or ion) bonded to surrounding ligands (molecules or anions). The ligands sacrifice the donor atoms (in the form of at least one pair of electrons) to the central atom. Many inorganic compounds are ionic, meaning they form ionic bonds rather than share electrons. They may have high melting points because of this. They may also be colorful, but this is not an absolute identifier of an inorganic compound. Salts, which are inorganic compounds, are an example of inorganic bonding of cations and anions. Some examples of salts are magnesium chloride ($MgCl_2$) and sodium oxide (Na_2O). Oxides, carbonates, sulfates, and halides are classes of inorganic compounds. They are typically poor conductors, are very water soluble, and crystallize easily. Minerals and silicates are also inorganic compounds.

Two of the main characteristics of organic compounds are that they include carbon and are formed by covalent bonds. Carbon can form long chains, double and triple bonds, and rings. While inorganic compounds tend to have high melting points, organic compounds tend to melt at temperatures below 300° C. They also tend to boil, sublimate, and decompose below this temperature. Unlike inorganic compounds, they are not very water soluble. Organic molecules are organized into functional groups based on their specific atoms, which helps determine how they will react chemically. A few groups are alkanes, nitro, alkenes, sulfides, amines, and carbolic acids. The hydroxyl group (-OH) consists of alcohols. These molecules are polar, which increases their solubility. By some estimates, there are more than 16 million organic compounds.

Nomenclature refers to the manner in which a compound is named. First, it must be determined whether the compound is ionic (formed through electron transfer between cations and anions) or molecular (formed through electron sharing between molecules). When dealing with an ionic compound, the name is determined using the standard naming conventions for ionic compounds. This involves indicating the positive element first (the charge must be defined when there is more than one option for the valency) followed by the negative element plus the appropriate suffix. The rules for naming a molecular compound are as follows: write elements in order of increasing group number and determine the prefix by determining the number of atoms. Exclude mono for the first atom. The name for CO_2, for example, is carbon dioxide. The end of oxygen is dropped and "ide" is added to make oxide, and the prefix "di" is used to indicate there are two atoms of oxygen.

Acids and Bases

The potential of hydrogen (pH) is a measurement of the concentration of hydrogen ions in a substance in terms of the number of moles of H^+ per liter of solution. A lower pH indicates a higher H^+ concentration, while a higher pH indicates a lower H^+ concentration. Pure water has a neutral pH, which is 7. Anything with a pH lower than water (less than 7) is considered acidic. Anything with a pH higher than water (greater than 7) is a base. Drain cleaner, soap, baking soda, ammonia, egg whites, and sea water are common bases. Urine, stomach acid, citric acid, vinegar, hydrochloric acid, and battery acid are acids. A pH indicator is a substance that acts as a detector of hydrogen or hydronium ions. It is halochromic, meaning it changes color to indicate that hydrogen or hydronium ions have been detected.

When they are dissolved in aqueous solutions, some properties of acids are that they conduct electricity, change blue litmus paper to red, have a sour taste, react with bases to neutralize them, and react with active metals to free hydrogen. A weak acid is one that does not donate all of its protons or disassociate completely. Strong acids include hydrochloric, hydriodic, hydrobromic, perchloric, nitric, and sulfuric. They ionize completely. Superacids are those that are stronger than 100 percent sulfuric acid. They include fluoroantimonic, magic, and perchloric acids. Acids can be used in pickling, a process used to remove rust and corrosion from metals. They are also used as catalysts in the processing of minerals and the production of salts and fertilizers. Phosphoric acid (H_3PO_4) is added to sodas and other acids are added to foods as preservatives or to add taste.

When they are dissolved in aqueous solutions, some properties of bases are that they conduct electricity, change red litmus paper to blue, feel slippery, and react with acids to neutralize their properties. A weak base is one that does not completely ionize in an aqueous solution, and usually has a low pH. Strong bases can free protons in very weak acids. Examples of strong bases are hydroxide compounds such as potassium, barium, and lithium hydroxides. Most are in the first and second groups of the periodic table. A superbase is extremely strong compared to sodium hydroxide and cannot be kept in an aqueous solution. Superbases are organized into organic, organometallic, and inorganic classes. Bases are used as insoluble catalysts in heterogeneous reactions and as catalysts in hydrogenation.

Some properties of salts are that they are formed from acid base reactions, are ionic compounds consisting of metallic and nonmetallic ions, dissociate in water, and are comprised of tightly bonded ions. Some common salts are sodium chloride (NaCl), sodium bisulfate, potassium dichromate ($K_2Cr_2O_7$), and calcium chloride ($CaCl_2$). Calcium chloride is used as a drying agent, and may be used to absorb moisture when freezing mixtures. Potassium nitrate (KNO_3) is used to make fertilizer and in the manufacture of explosives. Sodium nitrate ($NaNO_3$) is also used in the making of fertilizer. Baking soda (sodium bicarbonate) is a salt, as are Epsom salts [magnesium sulfate ($MgSO_4$)]. Salt and water can react to form a base and an acid. This is called a hydrolysis reaction.

A buffer is a solution whose pH remains relatively constant when a small amount of an acid or a base is added. It is usually made of a weak acid and its conjugate base (proton receiver) or one of its soluble salts. It can also be made of a weak base and its conjugate acid (proton donator) or one of its salts. A constant pH is necessary in living cells because some living things can only live within a certain pH range. If that pH changes, the cells could die. Blood is an example of a buffer. A pKa is a measure of acid dissociation or the acid dissociation constant. Buffer solutions can help keep enzymes at the correct pH. They are also used in the fermentation process, in dyeing fabrics, and in the calibration of pH meters. An example of a buffer is HC_2H_3O (a weak acid) and $NaC_2H_3O_2$ (a salt containing the $C_2H_3O_2^-$ ion).

General Concepts

Lewis formulas: These show the bonding or nonbonding tendency of specific pairs of valence electrons. Lewis dot diagrams use dots to represent valence electrons. Dots are paired around an atom. When an atom forms a covalent bond with another atom, the elements share the dots as they would electrons. Double and triple bonds are indicated with additional adjacent dots. Methane (CH_4), for instance, would be shown as a C with 2 dots above, below, and to the right and left and an H next to each set of dots. In structural formulas, the dots are single lines.

Kekulé diagrams: Like Lewis dot diagrams, these are two-dimensional representations of chemical compounds. Covalent bonds are shown as lines between elements. Double and triple bonds are shown as two or three lines and unbonded valence electrons are shown as dots.

Molar mass: This refers to the mass of one mole of a substance (element or compound), usually measured in grams per mole (g/mol). This differs from molecular mass in that molecular mass is the mass of one molecule of a substance relative to the atomic mass unit (amu).

Atomic mass unit (amu) is the smallest unit of mass, and is equal to 1/12 of the mass of the carbon isotope carbon-12. A mole (mol) is a measurement of molecular weight that is equal to the molecule's amu in grams. For example, carbon has an amu of 12, so a mole of carbon weighs 12 grams. One mole is equal to about 6.0221415×10^{23} elementary entities, which are usually atoms or molecules. This amount is also known as the Avogadro constant or Avogadro's number (NA). Another way to say this is that one mole of a substance is the same as one Avogadro's number of that substance. One mole of chlorine, for example, is 6.0221415×10^{23} chlorine atoms. The charge on one mole of electrons is referred to as a Faraday.

The kinetic theory of gases assumes that gas molecules are small compared to the distances between them and that they are in constant random motion. The attractive and repulsive forces between gas molecules are negligible. Their kinetic energy does not change with time as long as the temperature remains the same. The higher the temperature is, the greater the motion will be. As the temperature of a gas increases, so does the kinetic energy of the molecules. In other words, gas will occupy a greater volume as the temperature is increased and a lesser volume as the temperature is decreased. In addition, the same amount of gas will occupy a greater volume as the temperature increases, but pressure remains constant. At any given temperature, gas molecules have the same average kinetic energy. The ideal gas law is derived from the kinetic theory of gases.

Charles's law: This states that gases expand when they are heated. It is also known as the law of volumes.

Boyle's law: This states that gases contract when pressure is applied to them. It also states that if temperature remains constant, the relationship between absolute pressure and volume is inversely proportional. When one increases, the other decreases. Considered a specialized case of the ideal gas law, Boyle's law is sometimes known as the Boyle-Mariotte law.

The ideal gas law is used to explain the properties of a gas under ideal pressure, volume, and temperature conditions. It is best suited for describing monatomic gases (gases in which atoms are not bound together) and gases at high temperatures and low pressures. It is not well-suited for instances in which a gas or its components are close to their condensation point. All collisions are perfectly elastic and there are no intermolecular attractive forces at work. The ideal gas law is a way to explain and measure the macroscopic properties of matter. It can be derived from the kinetic theory of gases, which deals with the microscopic properties of matter. The equation for the ideal gas law is $PV = nRT$, where "P" is absolute pressure, "V" is absolute volume, and "T" is absolute temperature. "R" refers to the universal gas constant, which is 8.3145 J/mol Kelvin, and "n" is the number of moles.

Thermodynamics

Thermodynamics is a branch of physics that studies the conversion of energy into work and heat. It is especially concerned with variables such as temperature, volume, and pressure. Thermodynamic equilibrium refers to objects that have the same temperature because heat is transferred between them to reach equilibrium. Thermodynamics takes places within three different types of systems; open, isolated, and closed systems. Open systems are capable of interacting with a surrounding environment and can exchange heat, work (energy), and matter outside their system boundaries. A closed system can exchange heat and work, but not matter. An isolated system cannot exchange heat, work, or matter with its surroundings. Its total energy and mass stay the same. In physics, surrounding environment refers to everything outside a thermodynamic system (system). The terms "surroundings" and "environment" are also used. The term "boundary" refers to the division between the system and its surroundings.

The laws of thermodynamics are generalized principles dealing with energy and heat.
- The zeroth law of thermodynamics states that two objects in thermodynamic equilibrium with a third object are also in equilibrium with each other. Being in thermodynamic equilibrium basically means that different objects are at the same temperature.
- The first law deals with conservation of energy. It states that neither mass nor energy can be destroyed; only converted from one form to another.
- The second law states that the entropy (the amount of energy in a system that is no longer available for work or the amount of disorder in a system) of an isolated system can only increase. The second law also states that heat is not transferred from a lower-temperature system to a higher-temperature one unless additional work is done.
- The third law of thermodynamics states that as temperature approaches absolute zero, entropy approaches a constant minimum. It also states that a system cannot be cooled to absolute zero.

Thermal contact refers to energy transferred to a body by a means other than work. A system in thermal contact with another can exchange energy with it through the process of heat transfer. Thermal contact does not necessarily involve direct physical contact. Heat is energy that can be transferred from one body or system to another without work being done. Everything tends to become less organized and less useful over time (entropy). In all energy transfers, therefore, the overall result is that the heat is spread out so that objects are in thermodynamic equilibrium and the heat can no longer be transferred without additional work.

The laws of thermodynamics state that energy can be exchanged between physical systems as heat or work, and that systems are affected by their surroundings. It can be said that the total amount of energy in the universe is constant. The first law is mainly concerned with the conservation of energy and related concepts, which include the statement that energy can only be transferred or converted, not created or destroyed. The formula used to represent the first law is $\Delta U = Q - W$, where ΔU is the change in total internal energy of a system, Q is the heat added to the system, and W is the work done by the system. Energy can be transferred by conduction, convection, radiation, mass transfer, and other processes such as collisions in chemical and nuclear reactions. As transfers occur, the matter involved becomes less ordered and less useful. This tendency towards disorder is also referred to as entropy.

The second law of thermodynamics explains how energy can be used. In particular, it states that heat will not transfer spontaneously from a cold object to a hot object. Another way to say this is that heat transfers occur from higher temperatures to lower temperatures. Also covered under this law is the concept that systems not under the influence of external forces tend to become more disordered over time. This type of disorder can be expressed in terms of entropy. Another principle covered under this law is that it is impossible to make a heat engine that can extract heat and convert it all to useful work. A thermal bottleneck occurs in machines that convert energy to heat and then use it to do work. These types of machines are less efficient than ones that are solely mechanical.

Conduction is a form of heat transfer that occurs at the molecular level. It is the result of molecular agitation that occurs within an object, body, or material while the material stays motionless. An example of this is when a frying pan is placed on a hot burner. At first, the handle is not hot. As the pan becomes hotter due to conduction, the handle eventually gets hot too. In this example, energy is being transferred down the handle toward the colder end because the higher speed particles collide with and transfer energy to the slower ones. When this happens, the original material becomes cooler and the second material becomes hotter until equilibrium is reached. Thermal conduction can also occur between two substances such as a cup of hot coffee and the colder surface it is placed on. Heat is transferred, but matter is not.

Convection refers to heat transfer that occurs through the movement or circulation of fluids (liquids or gases). Some of the fluid becomes or is hotter than the surrounding fluid, and is less dense. Heat is transferred away from the source of the heat to a cooler, denser area. Examples of convection are boiling water and the movement of warm and cold air currents in the atmosphere and the ocean. Forced convection occurs in convection ovens, where a fan helps circulate hot air.

Radiation is heat transfer that occurs through the emission of electromagnetic waves, which carry energy away from the emitting object. All objects with temperatures above absolute zero radiate heat.

Temperature is a measurement of an object's stored heat energy. More specifically, temperature is the average kinetic energy of an object's particles. When the temperature of an object increases and its atoms move faster, kinetic energy also increases. Temperature is not energy since it changes and is not conserved. Thermometers are used to measure temperature.

There are three main scales for measuring temperature. Celsius uses the base reference points of water freezing at 0 degrees and boiling at 100 degrees. Fahrenheit uses the base reference points of water freezing at 32 degrees and boiling at 212 degrees. Celsius and Fahrenheit are both relative temperature scales since they use water as their reference point.

The Kelvin temperature scale is an absolute temperature scale. Its zero mark corresponds to absolute zero. Water's freezing and boiling points are 273.15 Kelvin and 373.15 Kelvin, respectively. Where Celsius and Fahrenheit are measured is degrees, Kelvin does not use degree terminology.

- Converting Celsius to Fahrenheit: $°F = \frac{9}{5}°C + 32$
- Converting Fahrenheit to Celsius: $°C = \frac{5}{9}(°F - 32)$
- Converting Celsius to Kelvin: $K = °C + 273.15$
- Converting Kelvin to Celsius: $°C = K - 273.15$

Heat capacity, also known as thermal mass, refers to the amount of heat energy required to raise the temperature of an object, and is measured in Joules per Kelvin or Joules per degree Celsius. The equation for relating heat energy to heat capacity is $Q = C\Delta T$, where Q is the heat energy transferred, C is the heat capacity of the body, and ΔT is the change in the object's temperature. Specific heat capacity, also known as specific heat, is the heat capacity per unit mass. Every element and compound has its own specific heat. For example, it takes different amounts of heat energy to raise the temperature of the same amounts of magnesium and lead by one degree. The equation for relating heat energy to specific heat capacity is $Q = mc\Delta T$, where m represents the mass of the object, and c represents its specific heat capacity.

Some discussions of energy consider only two types of energy: kinetic energy (the energy of motion) and potential energy (which depends on relative position or orientation). There are, however, other types of energy. Electromagnetic waves, for example, are a type of energy contained by a field. Another type of potential energy is electrical energy, which is the energy it takes to pull apart positive and negative electrical charges. Chemical energy refers to the manner in which atoms form into molecules, and this energy can be released or absorbed when molecules regroup. Solar energy comes in the form of visible light and non-visible light, such as infrared and ultraviolet rays. Sound energy refers to the energy in sound waves.

Energy is constantly changing forms and being transferred back and forth. An example of a heat to mechanical energy transformation is a steam engine, such as the type used on a steam locomotive. A heat source such as coal is used to boil water. The steam produced turns a shaft, which eventually turns the wheels. A pendulum swinging is an example of both a kinetic to potential and a potential to kinetic energy transformation. When a pendulum is moved from its center point (the point at which it is closest to the ground) to the highest point before it returns, it is an example of a kinetic to potential transformation. When it swings from its highest point toward the center, it is considered a potential to kinetic transformation. The sum of the potential and kinetic energy is known as the total mechanical energy. Stretching a rubber band gives it potential energy. That potential energy becomes kinetic energy when the rubber band is released.

Motion and Force

Mechanics is the study of matter and motion, and the topics related to matter and motion, such as force, energy, and work. Discussions of mechanics will often include the concepts of vectors and scalars. Vectors are quantities with both magnitude and direction, while scalars have only magnitude. Scalar quantities include length, area, volume, mass, density, energy, work, and power. Vector quantities include displacement, velocity, acceleration, momentum, and force.

Motion is a change in the location of an object, and is the result of an unbalanced net force acting on the object. Understanding motion requires the understanding of three basic quantities: displacement, velocity, and acceleration.

Displacement

When something moves from one place to another, it has undergone *displacement*. Displacement along a straight line is a very simple example of a vector quantity. If an object travels from position x = -5 cm to x = 5 cm, it has undergone a displacement of 10 cm. If it traverses the same path in the opposite direction, its displacement is -10 cm. A vector that spans the object's displacement in the direction of travel is known as a displacement vector.

Velocity

There are two types of velocity to consider: *average velocity* and *instantaneous velocity*. Unless an object has a constant velocity or we are explicitly given an equation for the velocity, finding the instantaneous velocity of an object requires the use of calculus. If we want to calculate the *average velocity* of an object, we need to know two things: the displacement, or the distance it has covered, and the time it took to cover this distance. The formula for average velocity is simply the distance traveled divided by the time required. In other words, the average velocity is equal to the change in position divided by the change in time. Average velocity is a vector and will always point in the same direction as the displacement vector (since time is a scalar and always positive).

Acceleration

Acceleration is the change in the velocity of an object. Typically, the acceleration will be a constant value. Like position and velocity, acceleration is a vector quantity and will therefore have both magnitude and direction.

Most motion can be explained by Newton's three laws of motion:

Newton's first law

An object at rest or in motion will remain at rest or in motion unless acted upon by an external force. This phenomenon is commonly referred to as inertia, the tendency of a body to remain in its present state of motion. In order for the body's state of motion to change, it must be acted on by an unbalanced force.

Newton's second law

An object's acceleration is directly proportional to the net force acting on the object, and inversely proportional to the object's mass. It is generally written in equation form $F = ma$, where F is the net force acting on a body, m is the mass of the body, and a is its acceleration. Note that since the mass is always a positive quantity, the acceleration is always in the same direction as the force.

Newton's third law

For every force, there is an equal and opposite force. When a hammer strikes a nail, the nail hits the hammer just as hard. If we consider two objects, A and B, then we may express any contact between these two bodies with the equation $F_{AB} = -F_{BA}$, where the order of the subscripts denotes which body is exerting the force. At first glance, this law might seem to forbid any movement at all since every force is being countered with an equal opposite force, but these equal opposite forces are acting on different bodies with different masses, so they will not cancel each other out.

Energy

The two types of energy most important in mechanics are potential and kinetic energy. Potential energy is the amount of energy an object has stored within itself because of its position or orientation. There are many types of potential energy, but the most common is gravitational potential energy. It is the energy that an object has because of its height (h) above the ground. It can be calculated as $PE = mgh$, where m is the object's mass and g is the acceleration of gravity. Kinetic energy is the energy of an object in motion, and is calculated as $KE = mv^2/2$, where v is the magnitude of its velocity. When an object is dropped, its potential energy is converted into kinetic energy as it falls. These two equations can be used to calculate the velocity of an object at any point in its fall.

Work

Work can be thought of as the amount of energy expended in accomplishing some goal. The simplest equation for mechanical work (W) is $W = Fd$, where F is the force exerted and d is the displacement of the object on which the force is exerted. This equation requires that the force be applied in the same direction as the displacement. If this is not the case, then the work may be calculated as $W = Fd \cos(\theta)$, where θ is the angle between the force and displacement vectors. If force and displacement have the same direction, then work is positive; if they are in opposite directions, then work is negative; and if they are perpendicular, the work done by the force is zero.

As an example, if a man pushes a block horizontally across a surface with a constant force of 10 N for a distance of 20 m, the work done by the man is 200 N-m or 200 J. If instead the block is sliding and the man tries to slow its progress by pushing against it, his work done is -200 J, since he is pushing in the direction opposite the motion. If the man pushes vertically downward on the block while it slides, his work done is zero, since his force vector is perpendicular to the displacement vector of the block.

Friction

Friction is a force that arises as a resistance to motion where two surfaces are in contact. The maximum magnitude of the frictional force (f) can be calculated as $f = F_c\mu$, where F_c is the contact force between the two objects and μ is a coefficient of friction based on the surfaces' material composition. Two types of friction are static and kinetic. To illustrate these concepts, imagine a book resting on a table. The force of its weight (W) is equal and opposite to the force of the table on the book, or the normal force (N). If we exert a small force (F) on the book, attempting to push it to one side, a frictional force (f) would arise, equal and opposite to our force. At this point, it is a *static frictional force* because the book is not moving. If we increase our force on the book, we will eventually cause it to move. At this point, the frictional force opposing us will be a *kinetic frictional force*. Generally, the kinetic frictional force is lower than static frictional force (because the frictional coefficient for static friction is larger), which means that the amount of force needed to maintain the movement of the book will be less than what was needed to start it moving.

Gravitational force

Gravitational force is a universal force that causes every object to exert a force on every other object. The gravitational force between two objects can be described by the formula, $F = Gm_1m_2/r^2$, where m_1 and m_2 are the masses of two objects, r is the distance between them, and G is the gravitational constant, $G = 6.672 \times 10^{-11}$ N-m^2/kg^2. In order for this force to have a noticeable effect, one or both of the objects must be extremely large, so the equation is generally only used in problems involving planetary bodies. For problems involving objects on the earth being affected by earth's gravitational pull, the force of gravity is simply calculated as $F = mg$, where g is 9.81 m/s^2 toward the ground.

Electrical force

Electrical force is a universal force that exists between any two electrically charged objects. Opposite charges attract one another and like charges repel one another. The magnitude of the force is directly proportional to the magnitude of the charges (q) and inversely proportional to the square of the distance (r) between the two objects: $F = kq_1q_2/r^2$, where $k = 9 \times 10^9$ N-m^2/C^2. Magnetic forces operate on a similar principle.

Buoyancy
The key determiner as to whether an object will float or sink in water is its density. The general rule is that if an object is less dense than water, it floats; if it is denser than water, it sinks. The density of an object is equal to its mass divided by its volume (d = m/v). It is important to note the difference between an object's density and a material's density. Water has a density of one gram per cubic centimeter, while steel has a density approximately eight times that. Despite having a much higher material density, an object made of steel may still float. A hollow steel sphere, for instance, will float easily because the density of the object includes the air contained within the sphere. An object may also float only in certain orientations. An ocean liner that is placed in the water upside down, for instance, may not remain afloat. An object will float only if it can displace a mass of water equal to its own mass.

Archimedes's principle states that a buoyant (upward) force on a submerged object is equal to the weight of the liquid displaced by the object. This principle of buoyancy can also be used to calculate the volume of an irregularly shaped object. The mass of the object (m) minus its apparent mass in the water (m_a) divided by the density of water (ρ_w), gives the object's volume: $V = (m - m_a)/\rho_w$.

Machines

Simple machines include the inclined plane, lever, wheel and axle, and pulley. These simple machines have no internal source of energy. More complex or compound machines can be formed from them. Simple machines provide a force known as a mechanical advantage and make it easier to accomplish a task. The inclined plane enables a force less than the object's weight to be used to push an object to a greater height. A lever enables a multiplication of force. The wheel and axle allows for movement with less resistance. Single or double pulleys allows for easier direction of force. The wedge and screw are forms of the inclined plane. A wedge turns a smaller force working over a greater distance into a larger force. The screw is similar to an incline that is wrapped around a shaft.

A certain amount of work is required to move an object. The amount cannot be reduced, but by changing the way the work is performed a mechanical advantage can be gained. A certain amount of work is required to raise an object to a given vertical height. By getting to a given height at an angle, the effort required is reduced, but the distance that must be traveled to reach a given height is increased. An example of this is walking up a hill. One may take a direct, shorter, but steeper route, or one may take a more meandering, longer route that requires less effort. Examples of wedges include doorstops, axes, plows, zippers, and can openers.

A lever consists of a bar or plank and a pivot point or fulcrum. Work is performed by the bar, which swings at the pivot point to redirect the force. There are three types of levers: first, second, and third class. Examples of a first-class lever include balances, see-saws, nail extractors, and scissors (which also use wedges). In a second-class lever the fulcrum is placed at one end of the bar and the work is performed at the other end. The weight or load to be moved is in between. The closer to the fulcrum the weight is, the easier it is to move. Force is increased, but the distance it is moved is decreased. Examples include pry bars, bottle openers, nutcrackers, and wheelbarrows. In a third-class lever the fulcrum is at one end and the positions of the weight and the location where the work is performed are reversed. Examples include fishing rods, hammers, and tweezers.

The center of a wheel and axle can be likened to a fulcrum on a rotating lever. As it turns, the wheel moves a greater distance than the axle, but with less force. Obvious examples of the wheel and axle are the wheels of a car, but this type of simple machine can also be used to exert a greater force. For instance, a person can turn the handles of a winch to exert a greater force at the turning axle to move an object. Other examples include steering wheels, wrenches, faucets, waterwheels, windmills, gears, and belts. Gears work together to change a force. The four basic types of gears are spur, rack and pinion, bevel, and worm gears. The larger gear turns slower than the smaller, but exerts a greater force. Gears at angles can be used to change the direction of forces.

A single pulley consists of a rope or line that is run around a wheel. This allows force to be directed in a downward motion to lift an object. This does not decrease the force required, just changes its direction. The load is moved the same distance as the rope pulling it. When a combination pulley is used, such as a double pulley, the weight is moved half the distance of the rope pulling it. In this way, the work effort is doubled. Pulleys are never 100% efficient because of friction. Examples of pulleys include cranes, chain hoists, block and tackles, and elevators.

Electrical Charges

A glass rod and a plastic rod can illustrate the concept of static electricity due to friction. Both start with no charge. A glass rod rubbed with silk produces a positive charge, while a plastic rod rubbed with fur produces a negative charge. The electron affinity of a material is a property that helps determine how easily it can be charged by friction. Materials can be sorted by their affinity for electrons into a triboelectric series. Materials with greater affinities include celluloid, sulfur, and rubber. Materials with lower affinities include glass, rabbit fur, and asbestos. In the example of a glass rod and a plastic one, the glass rod rubbed with silk acquires a positive charge because glass has a lower affinity for electrons than silk. The electrons flow to the silk, leaving the rod with fewer electrons and a positive charge. When a plastic rod is rubbed with fur, electrons flow to the rod and result in a negative charge.

The attractive force between the electrons and the nucleus is called the electric force. A positive (+) charge or a negative (-) charge creates a field of sorts in the empty space around it, which is known as an electric field. The direction of a positive charge is away from it and the direction of a negative charge is towards it. An electron within the force of the field is pulled towards a positive charge because an electron has a negative charge. A particle with a positive charge is pushed away, or repelled, by another positive charge. Like charges repel each other and opposite charges attract. Lines of force show the paths of charges. Electric force between two objects is directly proportional to the product of the charge magnitudes and inversely proportional to the square of the distance between the two objects. Electric charge is measured with the unit Coulomb (C). It is the amount of charge moved in one second by a steady current of one ampere ($1C = 1A \times 1s$).

Insulators are materials that prevent the movement of electrical charges, while conductors are materials that allow the movement of electrical charges. This is because conductive materials have free electrons that can move through the entire volume of the conductor. This allows an external charge to change the charge distribution in the material. In induction, a neutral conductive material, such as a sphere, can become charged by a positively or negatively charged object, such as a rod. The charged object is placed close to the material without touching it. This produces a force on the free electrons, which will either be attracted to or repelled by the rod, polarizing (or separating) the charge. The sphere's electrons will flow into or out of it when touched by a ground. The sphere is now charged. The charge will be opposite that of the charging rod.

Charging by conduction is similar to charging by induction, except that the material transferring the charge actually touches the material receiving the charge. A negatively or positively charged object is touched to an object with a neutral charge. Electrons will either flow into or out of the neutral object and it will become charged. Insulators cannot be used to conduct charges. Charging by conduction can also be called charging by contact. The law of conservation of charge states that the total number of units before and after a charging process remains the same. No electrons have been created. They have just been moved around. The removal of a charge on an object by conduction is called grounding.

Circuits

Electric potential, or electrostatic potential or voltage, is an expression of potential energy per unit of charge. It is measured in volts (V) as a scalar quantity. The formula used is $V = E/Q$, where V is voltage, E is electrical potential energy, and Q is the charge. Voltage is typically discussed in the context of electric potential difference between two points in a circuit. Voltage can also be thought of as a measure of the rate at which energy is drawn from a source in order to produce a flow of electric charge.

Electric current is the sustained flow of electrons that are part of an electric charge moving along a path in a circuit. This differs from a static electric charge, which is a constant non-moving charge rather than a continuous flow. The rate of flow of electric charge is expressed using the ampere (amp or A) and can be measured using an ammeter. A current of 1 ampere means that 1 coulomb of charge passes through a given area every second. Electric charges typically only move from areas of high electric potential to areas of low electric potential. To get charges to flow into a high potential area, you must to connect it to an area of higher potential, by introducing a battery or other voltage source.

Electric currents experience resistance as they travel through a circuit. Different objects have different levels of resistance. The ohm (Ω) is the measurement unit of electric resistance. The symbol is the Greek letter omega. Ohm's Law, which is expressed as $I = V/R$, states that current flow (I, measured in amps) through an object is equal to the potential difference from one side to the other (V, measured in volts) divided by resistance (R, measured in ohms). An object with a higher resistance will have a lower current flow through it given the same potential difference.

Movement of electric charge along a path between areas of high electric potential and low electric potential, with a resistor or load device between them, is the definition of a simple circuit. It is a closed conducting path between the high and low potential points, such as the positive and negative terminals on a battery. One example of a circuit is the flow from one terminal of a car battery to the other. The electrolyte solution of water and sulfuric acid provides work in chemical form to start the flow. A frequently used classroom example of circuits involves using a D cell (1.5 V) battery, a small light bulb, and a piece of copper wire to create a circuit to light the bulb.

Magnets

A magnet is a piece of metal, such as iron, steel, or magnetite (lodestone) that can affect another substance within its field of force that has like characteristics. Magnets can either attract or repel other substances. Magnets have two poles: north and south. Like poles repel and opposite poles (pairs of north and south) attract. The magnetic field is a set of invisible lines representing the paths of attraction and repulsion. Magnetism can occur naturally, or ferromagnetic materials can be magnetized. Certain matter that is magnetized can retain its magnetic properties indefinitely and become a permanent magnet. Other matter can lose its magnetic properties. For example, an iron nail can be temporarily magnetized by stroking it repeatedly in the same direction using one pole of another magnet. Once magnetized, it can attract or repel other magnetically inclined materials, such as paper clips. Dropping the nail repeatedly will cause it to lose its charge.

The motions of subatomic structures (nuclei and electrons) produce a magnetic field. It is the direction of the spin and orbit that indicate the direction of the field. The strength of a magnetic field is known as the magnetic moment. As electrons spin and orbit a nucleus, they produce a magnetic field. Pairs of electrons that spin and orbit in opposite directions cancel each other out, creating a net magnetic field of zero. Materials that have an unpaired electron are magnetic. Those with a weak attractive force are referred to as paramagnetic materials, while ferromagnetic materials have a strong attractive force. A diamagnetic material has electrons that are paired, and therefore does not typically have a magnetic moment. There are, however, some diamagnetic materials that have a weak magnetic field.

A magnetic field can be formed not only by a magnetic material, but also by electric current flowing through a wire. When a coiled wire is attached to the two ends of a battery, for example, an electromagnet can be formed by inserting a ferromagnetic material such as an iron bar within the coil. When electric current flows through the wire, the bar becomes a magnet. If there is no current, the magnetism is lost. A magnetic domain occurs when the magnetic fields of atoms are grouped and aligned. These groups form what can be thought of as miniature magnets within a material. This is what happens when an object like an iron nail is temporarily magnetized. Prior to magnetization, the organization of atoms and their various polarities are somewhat random with respect to where the north and south poles are pointing. After magnetization, a significant percentage of the poles are lined up in one direction, which is what causes the magnetic force exerted by the material.

Waves

Waves have energy and can transfer energy when they interact with matter. Although waves transfer energy, they do not transport matter. They are a disturbance of matter that transfers energy from one particle to an adjacent particle. There are many types of waves, including sound, seismic, water, light, micro, and radio waves. The two basic categories of waves are mechanical and electromagnetic. Mechanical waves are those that transmit energy through matter. Electromagnetic waves can transmit energy through a vacuum. A transverse wave provides a good illustration of the features of a wave, which include crests, troughs, amplitude, and wavelength.

There are a number of important attributes of waves. Frequency is a measure of how often particles in a medium vibrate when a wave passes through the medium with respect to a certain point or node. Usually measured in Hertz (Hz), frequency might refer to cycles per second, vibrations per second, or waves per second. One Hz is equal to one cycle per second.

Period is a measure of how long it takes to complete a cycle. It is the inverse of frequency; where frequency is measure in cycles per second, period can be thought of as seconds per cycle, though it is measured in units of time only.

Speed refers to how fast or slow a wave travels. It is measured in terms of distance divided by time. While frequency is measured in terms of cycles per second, speed might be measured in terms of meters per second.

Amplitude is the maximum amount of displacement of a particle in a medium from its rest position, and corresponds to the amount of energy carried by the wave. High-energy waves have greater amplitudes; low energy waves have lesser amplitudes. Amplitude is a measure of a wave's strength.

Rest position, also called equilibrium, is the point at which there is neither positive nor negative displacement. Crest, also called the peak, is the point at which a wave's positive or upward displacement from the rest position is at its maximum. Trough, also called a valley, is the point at which a wave's negative or downward displacement from the rest position is at its maximum. A wavelength is one complete wave cycle. It could be measured from crest to crest, trough to trough, rest position to rest position, or any point of a wave to the corresponding point on the next wave.

Sound is a pressure disturbance that moves through a medium in the form of mechanical waves, which transfer energy from one particle to the next. Sound requires a medium to travel through, such as air, water, or other matter since it is the vibrations that transfer energy to adjacent particles, not the actual movement of particles over a great distance. Sound is transferred through the movement of atomic particles, which can be atoms or molecules. Waves of sound energy move outward in all directions from the source. Sound waves consist of compressions (particles are forced together) and rarefactions (particles move farther apart and their density decreases). A wavelength consists of one compression and one rarefaction. Different sounds have different wavelengths. Sound is a form of kinetic energy.

The electromagnetic spectrum is defined by frequency (f) and wavelength (λ). Frequency is typically measured in hertz and wavelength is usually measured in meters. Because light travels at a fairly constant speed, frequency is inversely proportional to wavelength, a relationship expressed by the formula $f = c/\lambda$, where c is the speed of light (about 300 million meters per second). Frequency multiplied by wavelength equals the speed of the wave; for electromagnetic waves, this is the speed of light, with some variance for the medium in which it is traveling. Electromagnetic waves include (from largest to smallest wavelength) radio waves, microwaves, infrared radiation (radiant heat), visible light, ultraviolet radiation, x-rays, and gamma rays. The energy of electromagnetic waves is carried in packets that have a magnitude inversely proportional to the wavelength. Radio waves have a range of wavelengths, from about 10^{-3} to 10^5 meters, while their frequencies range from 10^3 to about 10^{11} Hz.

Atoms and molecules can gain or lose energy only in particular, discrete amounts. Therefore, they can absorb and emit light only at wavelengths that correspond to these amounts. Using a process known as spectroscopy, these characteristic wavelengths can be used to identify substances.

Light is the portion of the electromagnetic spectrum that is visible because of its ability to stimulate the retina. It is absorbed and emitted by electrons, atoms, and molecules that move from one energy level to another. Visible light interacts with matter through molecular electron excitation (which occurs in the human retina) and through plasma oscillations (which occur in metals). Visible light is between ultraviolet and infrared light on the spectrum. The wavelengths of visible light cover a range from 380 nm (violet) to 760 nm (red). Different wavelengths correspond to different colors.

The human brain interprets or perceives visible light, which is emitted from the sun and other stars, as color. For example, when the entire wavelength reaches the retina, the brain perceives the color white. When no part of the wavelength reaches the retina, the brain perceives the color black. The particular color of an object depends upon what is absorbed and what is transmitted or reflected. For example, a leaf consists of chlorophyll molecules, the atoms of which absorb all wavelengths of the visible light spectrum except for green, which is why a leaf appears green. Certain wavelengths of visible light can be absorbed when they interact with matter. Wavelengths that are not absorbed can be transmitted by transparent materials or reflected by opaque materials.

When light waves encounter an object, they are either reflected, transmitted, or absorbed. If the light is reflected from the surface of the object, the angle at which it contacts the surface will be the same as the angle at which it leaves, on the other side of the perpendicular. If the ray of light is perpendicular to the surface, it will be reflected back in the direction from which it came. When light is transmitted through the object, its direction may be altered upon entering the object. This is known as refraction. When light waves are refracted, or bent, an image can appear distorted. The degree to which the light is refracted depends on the speed at which light travels in the object. Light that is neither reflected nor transmitted will be absorbed by the surface and stored as heat energy. Nearly all instances of light hitting an object will involve a combination of two or even all three of these.

Diffraction refers to the bending of waves around small objects and the spreading out of waves past small openings. The narrower the opening, the greater the level of diffraction will be. Larger wavelengths also increase diffraction. A diffraction grating can be created by placing a number of slits close together, and is used more frequently than a prism to separate light. Different wavelengths are diffracted at different angles.

The various properties of light have numerous real life applications. For example, polarized sunglasses have lenses that help reduce glare, while non-polarized sunglasses reduce the total amount of light that reaches the eyes. Polarized lenses consist of a chemical film of molecules aligned in parallel. This allows the lenses to block wavelengths of light that are intense, horizontal, and reflected from smooth, flat surfaces. The "fiber" in fiber optics refers to a tube or pipe that channels light. Because of the composition of the fiber, light can be transmitted greater distances before losing the signal. The fiber consists of a core, cladding, and a coating. Fibers are bundled, allowing for the transmission of large amounts of data.

Social Sciences

U.S. Constitution

The U.S. Constitution represents the highest law within the United States. It was the successor of the Articles of Confederation and was finished in 1787, adopted by the Constitutional Convention in Philadelphia, and subsequently ratified by the thirteen original states. The U.S. Constitution established a federal union of sovereign states, as well as a federal government to oversee the union. The U.S. Constitution went into effect in 1789 and has been a model for constitutions created within other nations. The Fourteenth Amendment of the Constitution provides all United States citizens with equal protection under the Constitution. The judiciary branch of the federal government has the power to review the constitutionality of laws passed in the United States and can strike down laws if they are determined to be unconstitutional. The Fifth Article of the Constitution addresses how Congress may propose Constitutional amendments. In addition, a convention consisting of at least two thirds of the states can propose Constitutional amendments. Amendments must be ratified before they become part of the Constitution.

Governing principles
The governing principles of the United State Constitution include the principle of popular sovereignty, which is associated with a system of government is created by the people, for the people. Other governing principles of the United State Constitution include the rule of law, the Supreme Court, judicial review, the separation of powers, and the system of checks and balances. In addition, the governing principle of federalism guided the formulation of the United States Constitution, allowing for sharing of power between the federal government and the states. The governing principles of the Constitution also included individual rights, which are embodied in the Bill of Rights.

Influential documents
There are a number of documents that influenced the writing of the United States Constitution. These include the Magna Carta, which was written in 1215 A.D. and represented the English liberty charter. In addition, the Mayflower Compact was influential; it was written in 1620 by the first settlers in the New England colony. The Virginia Declaration of Rights was written in 1776 and served as a prototype for other state constitutions and for the Bill of Rights. The Declaration of Independence was also adopted in 1776 and was influential in the writing of the Constitution. The Articles of Confederation was adopted in 1781 and served as the first constitution for the original thirteen states following the American Revolution. The Federalist Papers also served as an influence for the drafters of the U.S. Constitution; they were published in newspapers to encourage ratification of the Constitution, which was ratified in 1788.

Bill of Rights

The Bill of Rights includes the first ten amendments to the Constitution. These amendments were proposed to the states by the first Congress of the United States of America as a means to protect personal and civil liberties. The Bill of Rights was originally composed of twelve amendments, which were proposed by Congress on September 25, 1789. In 1791, the group of ten amendments that comprise what is known as the Bill of Rights was ratified by the states. These amendments became part of the Constitution of the United States.

The First Amendment protects the five most important civil liberties of citizens of the United States. These civil liberties include the freedom of religion, the freedom of speech, the freedom of the press, the right of assembly, and the freedom to petition. The Second Amendment protects the right to bear arms. The Third Amendment protects the right of citizens not to have troops placed in their private homes. The Fourth Amendment protects citizens against search and seizure of their private homes without a warrant. The Fifth Amendment pertains to the rights of an accused person and protects the right to a trial, the right not to be tried twice for the same crime (double jeopardy), and the right against self incrimination. The Fifth Amendment also protects the right of citizens against the taking of their private property without just compensation.

Reconstruction Amendments

The Thirteenth, Fourteenth and Fifteenth Amendments are known as the Reconstruction Amendments. They are grouped together in this manner because they were passed during the Reconstruction period following the Civil War. They were drafted with the purpose of abolishing slavery, preventing slavery under other names, and extending rights to all citizens of the United States, regardless of race or color. Specifically, the Thirteenth Amendment, which was ratified in 1865, abolished slavery in the United States. The Fourteenth Amendment, which was ratified in 1868, established limitations on states such that no state may deny any citizen equal protection under the laws. The Fifteenth Amendment, which was ratified in 1870, established the right of citizens to vote regardless of race or color.

Nineteenth Amendment

The Nineteenth Amendment gave women the right to vote. This amendment was proposed on June 4, 1919 and was ratified on August 18, 1920. An amendment to give women the right to vote was first introduced in Congress in 1878, but it failed to pass. For the next four decades, the amendment was reintroduced in every session of Congress but was defeated each time. The involvement of women in the war effort during World War I spawned increased support for women's suffrage. Finally, in 1918, the House of Representatives approved the amendment to grant women suffrage, but the Senate defeated it. In 1919, the Senate also passed the amendment and sent it to the states for approval, where it was ratified in 1920.

25th Amendment

If the Presidency is vacated, the Vice President becomes President. If the Vice Presidency is vacated, the President nominates a Vice President, who must be approved by a majority vote in Congress. If the President informs Congress that he is unable to execute the powers and duties of the Presidency, the Vice President assumes the Presidency until the President informs Congress that he is able to return to office. Similarly, the Vice President will assume the Presidency if the Vice President and a majority of the Cabinet inform Congress that the President is unable to serve as President, and the President may resume office if he informs Congress that he is able to do so. The Vice President and the Cabinet can counter the President's assertion that he is able to resume office and by a two thirds vote within Congress the Vice President will continue to act as President.

Articles of Confederation

The very first constitution in the history of the United States was the Articles of Confederation. The Articles of Confederation served as a plan for the government of the United States and was created on the principles that were defended during the Revolutionary War. However, the Articles of

Confederation contained weaknesses. Specifically, the Articles of Confederation did not assign the power to create and collect taxes, did not assign power to oversee trade, and it created a relatively weak executive power without the ability to enforce legislation. The greatest fault of the Articles of Confederation was that it did not originate with the people, but rather power was vested in the states to avoid a central government authority. Under the Articles of Confederation, every state could collect its own taxes, issue currency, and maintain its own militia, creating inefficiencies in the national government. The national government was primarily responsible for foreign policy and treaties. The Articles of Confederation provides learning opportunities and was a stepping stone in creating the Constitution.

U.S. President

<u>Term and qualifications</u>
The President of the United States is elected for a term of four years. The President may serve for a maximum of two terms. In order to be the President of the United States of America, an individual must be a natural born citizen of the United States. Candidates for the position of United States President must also be at least thirty-five years of age. Finally, in order to become President of the United States of America, an individual must have been a resident of the United States for at least fourteen years.

<u>Powers</u>
The President of the U.S. is the Head of the Executive Branch. The powers of the President are defined by the U.S. Constitution, and include the power to act as Commander in Chief of U.S. Armed Forces; as such, the President can authorize the use of troops without a declaration of war. To declare war, the President must receive approval from Congress. The President must also receive the consent of Congress when using the power to make treaties, appoint the heads of Executive Branch departments, and appoint ambassadors, Supreme Court judges, federal judges, and other officials. The President also has the power to receive foreign ambassadors and other representatives of foreign nations; to provide a yearly State of the Union Address; to recommend legislation; to convene and adjourn Congress; to ensure that laws are carried out; to fill administrative openings when Congress is in recess; and to issue reprieves and pardons for crimes against the United States.

The President can recommend legislation to members of Congress, who can then introduce it as a bill. Only Congress can create legislation, but the President's approval of a bill is significant in determining whether it will pass. The President may sign a bill into law, veto a bill, or do nothing with it once it has passed Congress and been sent to the President for approval. If the President signs a bill into law, only the Supreme Court can then dismiss it by finding it unconstitutional. If a bill is vetoed, it is sent back to Congress without the President's signature, where Congress can override the veto with two-thirds approval. If the President does nothing with a bill, and Congress is in session ten business days following the receipt of the bill by the President, it becomes law without the President's signature; if Congress adjourns within ten business days, the bill dies, which is referred to as a pocket veto. The President can only veto a bill in its entirety.

Legislative Branch

The Legislative branch was established by Article I of the United States Constitution. The Legislative branch is responsible for making laws. In the United States the Legislative branch is a bicameral system, which means that it is divided into two houses, the House of Representatives and the Senate. The bicameral system ensures that checks and balances exist within the Legislative branch.

Representatives and Senators are elected by the people in the state that they represent. Also included in the Legislative branch are all of the agencies that provide support to Congress, including the Government Printing Office, the Library of Congress, the Congressional Budget Office, the General Accounting Office, and the Architect of the Capitol.

Congress

The Congress represents one part of the legislative branch in the United States. Congress is composed of two chambers known as the House of Representatives and the Senate. The two chamber system is referred to as a bicameral legislative system. Congress is responsible for writing, debating, and passing bills. Once bills are passed by Congress, they go to the President of the United States to be reviewed, approved and signed into law. Congress is also responsible for investigating issues that are important on a national level and for overseeing both the executive and judicial branches. Elections are held every two years for all 435 members of the House of Representatives and for one third of the members of the Senate. Congress begins a new session every January after Congressional elections. Congress convenes once a year, typically from January 3rd through July 31st.

Article I Section 8 of the Constitution gives Congress the power to establish and collect taxes; to pay debts; to provide for the defense of the country; to borrow money on credit; to regulate domestic and international commerce; to establish immigration policy; to establish bankruptcies laws; to create money; to establish a postal system; to protect patents and intellectual property rights; to create lower courts; to control and protect citizens and ships in international waters; to declare war; to establish and maintain an army and a navy; to maintain National Guard readiness; and to exercise control over the District of Columbia and other federal property. Section 8 also includes a clause known as the Elastic Clause which gives Congress the power to pass any law necessary for carrying out the actions over which it has power.

House of Representatives

There are 435 members of the House of Representatives. Every member represents a region within a state; these regions are referred to as congressional districts and are based on population size. Congressional districts are established every ten years through the process of a population census which is carried out by the U.S. Census Bureau. The number of congressional districts in a state determines how many Representatives are from that state. Every state has at least one seat in the House. Representatives come not only from the fifty states but in addition five members represent Puerto Rico, Guam, American Samoa, the Virgin Islands, and D.C. These five members are not permitted to vote in Congress, but are permitted to engage in debates. The House is solely responsible for initiating laws that require citizens to pay taxes and for determining whether government officials should be tried for committing crimes against the U.S.

The Senate

There are 100 members of the United States Senate. The U.S. Constitution stipulates that the Vice President of the United States controls the Senate and is therefore referred to as the president of the Senate. However, in reality the Vice President is not regularly in attendance when the Senate is in session; rather, the Vice President is typically only in attendance during significant ceremonial events and when he is required to vote to break a tie within the Senate. The Senate is solely responsible for either confirming or disapproving of treaties that are drafted by the United States President. The Senate is also solely responsible for either confirming or disapproving of appointments made by the United States President, including Cabinet-level appointments, officers, Supreme Court judges, and ambassadors. In addition, the Senate is solely responsible for trying government officials who commit crimes against the United States.

Bills

A bill is a piece of legislation that is formally introduces in Congress. A bill can originate in either the House of Representatives or in the Senate. When a bill originates in the House of Representatives it is designated as H.R. When a bill originates in the Senate it is designated by S. Bills are numbered in consecutive order. Bills can be categorized into either public bills or private bills. Public bills address general issues. If a public bill is both approved by Congress and signed by the President it is passed and it becomes a Public Law, or a Public Act. In contrast, private bills address individual circumstances. For example, private bills might be introduced to address a case against the Federal Government, immigration and naturalization cases, or land titles. If a private bill is both approved by Congress and signed by the President it is passed and it becomes a private law.

Judicial Branch

The United States Judicial Branch was established with the creation of the U.S. Supreme Court, which was stipulated by Article III of the U.S. Constitution. The Supreme Court is the highest court in the United States and it is granted the judicial powers of the United States government. In addition to the Supreme Court, the judicial branch also consists of lower Federal courts that were created by Congress using its Constitutional powers. The responsibility of the Courts is to settle disputes about the meaning of laws and how laws are applied, and through judicial review to decide whether or not laws violate the U.S. Constitution. It is through judicial review that the judicial branch exercises the system of checks and balances with regard to the executive and legislative branches.

Powers of the Supreme Court

The Supreme Court is the highest court. The Supreme Court's is tasked with settling disputes involving the interpretation of the Constitution. The process of determining whether a law or action is in violation of the Constitution is judicial review. The Supreme Court can overturn both state and federal laws if they are determined to violate the Constitution. The decisions of the Supreme Court can only be altered by means of another Supreme Court decision or through an amendment to the Constitution. The Supreme Court has full authority over federal courts and restricted authority over state courts. The Supreme Court has the final say over cases heard by federal courts, and also stipulates the procedures that federal courts must abide by. Although federal courts are required to uphold the Supreme Court's interpretations of federal laws and the Constitution and the Supreme Court's interpretations of federal law and the Constitution also apply to state courts, the Supreme Court cannot interpret state laws or Constitutions and doesn't oversee state court procedures.

Supreme Court Justices

Nine Justices currently comprise the Supreme Court; eight of these are referred to as Associate Justices and one is referred to as the Chief Justice. The number of Supreme Court Justices is set by Congress. The Supreme Court Justices are appointed by the President of the United States and with consent from the Senate. After individuals have been approved by the Senate and have been sworn in to the Supreme Court, they may keep the position of Supreme Court Justice for the remainder of their lives. Justices may leave their positions if they choose to resign or retire, or if they die, or if they are impeached. Historically, there has never been a Justice who has been removed from the Supreme Court through impeachment. There are not any specific requirements to become a Supreme Court Justice.

State versus federal government

Initially, government systems in the United States were characterized as state governments that were essentially self-governed. These circumstances in the early days of the United States represented an aversion to the centralized government that was present in England, the colonial power that first controlled America. The state government system proved to be insufficient and therefore the Constitution was written to delineate the powers afforded to a federal government. The Constitution also delineates the relationship between the federal and state governments. The system instituted in the Constitution is a known as a federalist system, in which powers are shared between the federal and state governments. Specific powers are allocated to the federal government, while other powers remain in the hands of state governments.

Concurrent powers

While both the national and state governments reserve specific powers that the other does not have, there are certain powers that are shared between the national and state governments. These shared powers are known as concurrent powers. The concurrent powers that are shared by both the national government and the state governments include the power to collect taxes, the power to build roads, the power to borrow money, the power to create courts, the power to create and enforce laws, the power to establish banks and corporations, the power to spend funds in the interest of the general welfare of the United States and its citizens, and the power to take private property for purposes that benefit the public so long as just compensation is provided.

State constitutions

In the United States, state governments each have a unique state constitution. State constitutions resemble the federal Constitution in many ways. However, state constitutions may not be in disaccord with the federal Constitution. State governments have control over affairs that occur within state boundaries, such as communications within state boundaries, regulations concerning property, industry, business, and public utilities, criminal codes, and labor conditions. There are also numerous matters over which state and federal government shares jurisdiction. State constitutions differ from one another with regard to some issues, but typically they all are laid out similarly to the federal Constitution. All state constitutions contain a section on people's rights and a section that outlines how government should be organized. Every state constitution also stipulates that ultimate authority rests with the people and establishes specific standards and values as the basis of government.

State executive and legislative branches

State governments are divided into executive, legislative, and judicial branches, just as in the federal government. In a state government, the governor serves as the head of the executive branch. The governor is elected by popular vote for a term of either two or four years depending on the state. Every state in the U.S. has a bicameral legislature except Nebraska, which has a single legislative body. The bicameral legislature is divided into an upper house and a lower house. The upper house is typically referred to as the Senate, as in the federal government, and the lower house can be referred to by a number of names, including the House of Representatives, the House of Delegates, or the General Assembly. State senators typically serve for a term of four years, while members of the House of Representatives, House of Delegates or the General Assembly serve for a term of two years.

State and local courts

Every state has a court system that is independent and distinct from the federal court system. The hierarchy of the state court system includes trial courts at the lowest level; appellate courts are the highest courts in the state court system. The great majority, over ninety-five percent, of the court cases in the United States are heard and decided in state courts and local courts, which also fall under the jurisdiction of the states. Depending on the state, there may be one or two appellate courts within the state. States organize and name their courts differently. Typically, lower courts are assigned specific names and authority to hear specific types of cases, such as family courts and probate courts. Beneath the specialized trial courts are more informal trial courts, including magistrate courts and justice of the peace courts, which typically do not involve a jury.

City government

Approximately eighty percent of the population in the United States resides in urban areas or areas immediately surrounding urban areas. Therefore, city governments are an integral part of the general system of government within the United States. City governments provide direct services to their citizens even more so than the federal government or state governments. Examples of services that are provided by city governments include police forces and firefighting forces, health and sanitation, education, public transportation, and housing. City governments are chartered by state governments; the city charter outlines the objectives and powers allocated to the city. While many city governments operate independently from state governments, many large cities work in collaboration with state and federal government. The organization of city governments varies, but the majority have a central council that is chosen by the people through an election, as well as an executive officer who is aided by department heads. Traditionally, there are mayor-council city governments, commission city governments, and city manager city governments.

County government

A county is a sub region within a state. Counties typically consist of at least two towns and a number of villages. Usually a single city or town within a county is named as the county seat. The county seat serves as the site at which government offices are situated. The county seat is also where the board of commissioners for the county convenes. Small counties have boards which are selected by the entire county. In contrast, large counties have commissioners who represent each town, city or district within the county. County boards are responsible for setting county taxes, appropriating funds, setting pay rates for county personnel, overseeing county elections, building and upkeep of highways and bridges, and managing federal, state, and county social welfare programs.

Town and village government

Many governments are too tiny to be classified as city governments. Such small jurisdictions are known as towns and villages and receive a charter from a state. Town and village governments address only local matters such as maintaining local roads, illuminating local roads, managing a local water supply, maintaining local police and firefighting forces, developing and implementing local health policies, providing or organizing the disposal of waste locally, setting local taxes, and managing local schools. Town and village governments are typically overseen by a board or a council that is chosen through election. A chairperson or a president can serve as the chief executive officer of the board or council. Alternatively, an elected mayor can serve as the chief executive officer of the board or council. Town and village governments can be staffed by clerks, treasurers, police and fire officers, and health and welfare officers.

Town meetings

Some local governments hold what are referred to as town meetings. Town meetings have occurred for more than two hundred years. The townships that hold town meetings are typically found throughout New England states. Town meetings are a rather unique characteristic that distinguishes some small town from other forms of government. Town meetings are typically held on an annual basis, but they can be held more often if necessary. At a town meeting, registered voters assemble in an open meeting to elect officers, discuss local matters, and vote on local legislation that concerns the operation of the local government. The attendees of the town meeting make decisions together as a community concerning issues such as road maintenance, building public facilities, tax rates, and town budgets.

Political parties

A political party is an organization that advocates a particular ideology and seeks to gain power within government. The tendency of members of political parties to support their party's policies and interests relative to those of other parties is referred to as partisanship. Often, a political party is comprised of members whose positions, interests and perspectives on policies vary, despite having shared interests in the general ideology of the party. As such, many political parties will have divisions within them that have differing opinions on policy. Political parties are often placed on a political spectrum, with one end of the spectrum representing conservative, traditional values and policies and the other end of the spectrum representing radical, progressive value and policies.

Party systems

There is a variety of party systems, including single-party systems, dominant-party systems, and dual-party systems. In a single-party system, only one political party may hold power. In this type of system, minor parties may be permitted, but they must accept the leadership of the dominant party. Dominant-party systems allow for multiple parties in opposition of one another; however the dominant party is the only party considered to have power. A two-party system, such as in the United States, is one in which there are two dominant political parties. In such a system, it is very difficult for any other parties to win an election. In most two-party systems, there is typically one right wing party and one left wing party.

Right-wing and left-wing political parties

Right-wing political parties in the United States of America are typically associated with conservatism or Christian democracy. Right-wing political parties and politics are considered to be the opposite of left-wing political parties and politics. In the United States of America, the Republican Party is the dominant right-wing political party. Left-wing political parties are typically associated with socialism, social democracy, or liberalism. Left-wing political parties and politics are considered to be the opposite of right-wing political parties and politics. In the United States of America, the Democratic Party is the dominant left-wing political party.

Democratic Party
The Democratic Party was founded in 1792. In the United States, it is one of the two dominant political parties, along with the Republican Party. The Democratic Party is to the left of the

Republican Party. The Democratic Party began as a conservative party in the mid-1800s, shifting to the left during the 1900s. There are many factions within the Democratic Party in the United States. The Democratic National Committee (DNC) is the official organization of the Democratic Party, and it develops and promotes the party's platform and coordinates fundraising and election strategies. There are Democratic committees in every U.S. state and most U.S. counties. The official symbol of the Democratic Party is the donkey.

Republican Party

The Republican Party is often referred to as the GOP, which stands for Grand Old Party. The Republican Party is considered socially conservative and economically neoliberal relative to the Democratic Party. Like the Democratic Party, there are factions within the Republic Party that agree with the party's overall ideology, but disagree with the party's positions on specific issues. The official symbol of the Republican Party is the elephant. The Republican National Committee (RNC) is the official organization of the Republican Party, and it develops and promotes the party's platform and coordinates fundraising and election strategies. There are Republican committees in every U.S. state and most U.S. counties.

Political campaigns

A political campaign is an organized attempt to influence the decisions of a particular group of people. Examples of campaigns could include elections or efforts to influence policy changes. One of the first steps in a campaign is to develop a campaign message. The message must then be delivered to the individuals and groups that the campaign is trying to reach and influence through a campaign plan. There are various ways for a campaign to communicate its message to the intended audience, including public media; paid media such as television, radio and newspaper ads, billboards and the internet; public events such as protests and rallies; meetings with speakers; mailings; canvassing; fliers; and websites. Through these efforts, the campaign attempts to attract additional support and, ultimately, to reach the goal of the campaign.

Campaign elements

Money is a significant aspect of a campaign because with changes in technology, campaigns have become increasingly expensive to run. Some of the costs associated with running a campaign include TV advertisements, mailings, and campaign staff salaries. Fundraising is often used to generate money to cover campaign costs. The capital that is necessary to run a campaign refers to human capital, which may consist of paid staff, volunteers, or a combination of both. Key members of a campaign include a campaign manager, people to make strategic decisions, and people to canvass door-to-door and make phone calls.

Voting

Voting is a method of decision making that allows people to express their opinion or preference for a candidate or for a proposed resolution of an issue. In a democratic system, voting typically takes place as part of an election. An individual participates in the voting process by casting a vote, or a ballot; ballots are produced by states. A secret ballot can be used at polls to protect voters' privacy. Individuals can also vote via absentee ballot. In some states voters can write-in a name to cast a vote for a candidate that is not on the ballot. Some states also use straight ticket voting, allowing the voter to vote for one party for all the elected positions on the ballot.

<u>Voting systems</u>
Different types of voting systems exist in the United States of America. In a single vote system, the voter can only vote for one option, precluding the voter from voting for anyone else. Alternatively, in a multiple vote system, the voter may vote for multiple options. In a ranked vote system, a voter may rank alternative options in order of preference. In a scored, or rated, vote system, the voter gives each option a score that falls on a scale between one and whatever number represents the upper boundary of the scale.

Elections in the United States

In the United States, officials are elected at the federal, state and local levels. The first two articles of the Constitution, as well as various amendments, establish how federal elections are to be held. The President is elected indirectly, by electors of an electoral college. Members of the electoral college nearly always vote along the lines of the popular vote of their respective states. Members of Congress are directly elected. At the state level, state law establishes most aspects of how elections are held. There are many elected offices at the state level, including a governor and state legislature. There are also elected offices at the local level.

Voter eligibility

The United States Constitution establishes that individual people are permitted to vote in elections if they are citizens of the United States and are at least eighteen years old. The fifteenth and nineteenth amendments of the United States Constitution stipulate that the right to vote cannot be denied to any United States citizen based on race or sex, respectively. States regulate voter eligibility beyond the minimum qualifications stipulated by the United States Constitution. Depending on the regulations of individual states, individuals may be denied the right to vote if they are convicted criminals.

Primaries and caucuses

Candidates for federal office are chosen by primaries and caucuses. In a primary election, voters in a jurisdiction choose a political party's candidate for a later election. Candidate for state level offices are also selected through primaries. The purpose of a caucus is also to nominate candidates for a later election. A caucus is a meeting that takes place in a precinct with the purpose of discussing each party's platform and voting issues such as voter turnout. Eleven states hold caucuses. The period of time known as the primary season in Presidential elections, which includes both primaries and caucuses, lasts from the Iowa caucus in January to the last primary, ends in early summer.

Political media

The political media includes forms of the media that are owned and overseen and managed by, or influenced by, political entities. The purpose of the political media is to disseminate the views and platforms of the associated political entity. The media is often referred to as a fourth power, in addition to the executive, legislative and judicial branches of the government. The internet is considered by some to be a form of political media. However, the internet is not completely identifiable as a political medium, given the lack of a central authority and the lack of a common political method of communication via the internet.

Petition

A petition is a request to an authority, most commonly a government official or public office or agency. A petition typically takes the form of a document that is addressed to an official who holds authority and that is signed by multiple individuals. In addition to written petitions, people may submit oral petitions, and today petitions are often internet-based. The First Amendment to the U.S. Constitution contains a clause known as the Petition Clause, which guarantees the right "to petition the Government for a redress of grievances." The right to petition includes the right to file lawsuits against the government. Petitions can be used for many purposes. One example includes petitions to qualify candidates for public office to appear on a ballot; in order for a candidate's name to appear on a ballot, the candidate must collect signatures from voters. Other types of petitions include those used in efforts to generate support for various causes.

Protest

A protest is an expression of opposition, and sometimes of support, to events or circumstances. Protests represent a means for individuals to publicly make their views heard in an effort to influence public opinion or government policy, or a means to enact change. Protests generally result when self expression of opposing views is restricted by government policy, political or economic circumstances, religion, social structures, or the media, and people react by declaring their views through cultural mechanisms or on the streets. There are numerous forms of protest, including boycotts, civil disobedience, demonstrations, non-violent protests, picketing, protest marches, protest songs, riots, sit-ins, teach-ins, strikes, and others.

Liberalism

Liberalism is an ideology based on the autonomy of individuals. Liberalism favors civil and political liberties, and seeks to maximize those liberties under law and ensure protection from arbitrary authority. A system characterized by liberalism would possess a pluralistic liberal democratic system of government, a rule of law, the free exchange of ideas, and economic competition. The basic principles of liberalism include transparency, individual and civil rights, particularly the right to life, liberty, and property, equal rights for all citizens under law, and government by the consent of the governed, which is guaranteed through elections. Liberalism also favors laissez-faire economics, the free market, and the gold standard.

Libertarianism

Libertarianism is an ideology that seeks to maximize individual rights, private property rights, and free market capitalism. Individuals who subscribe to the ideology of libertarianism believe that people should have the freedom to do what they will with their bodies and their private property as long as they do not coerce others to do the same. They also believe that individuals should have the liberty to make their own moral choices as long as they do not use coercion to prevent others from exercising the same liberty, and that government should not prevent an individual from making a moral choice or impose moral obligations on people. Libertarians advocate minimum government involvement except to protect liberty and prevent coercion. In addition, libertarians support capitalism and oppose social welfare, and also oppose government spending and programming that are not aimed at protecting liberty.

American liberalism

American liberalism is a political ideology which is derived from classical liberalism. Like classical liberalism, American liberalism is defined by the ideal of individual liberty. However, American liberalism typically rejects laissez faire economics and instead advocates for the creation and maintenance of institutions that foster social and economic equity. American liberalism began in the beginning of the twentieth century, and started to decline in the 1970s. American liberalism features support for government social programs, increased funding for public education, labor unions, regulation of business, civil rights, voting rights, reproductive rights, strong environmental regulations, public transportation, minimum wage requirements, government funding to alternative energy research, animal rights, gun control, and a progressive tax system. People who subscribe to American liberalism oppose the death penalty.

Nationalism

Nationalism is an ideology based upon the ideal that identification with a nation, ethnicity or nationality is an essential and defining part of human social existence. Nationalism is thus a universal ideology. However, nationalism also refers to the ideology that one national identity is superior to others, and to the view that nations benefit from acting independently rather than collectively. This view of nationalism often spawns nationalist movements, which make political claims on behalf of particular nations. Nationalists differentiate between nations based on specific criteria, and also differentiate between individual people based on which nation they are a member of. The criteria used to define national identity include ethnicity, a common language, a common culture, and common values. Nationalism has had an extremely significant impact on world history and geopolitics since the nation-state has become the prevailing form of state. Most people in the world currently live in states which are nation-states.

Conservatism

Conservatism is a political ideology that is founded on traditional values, a distrust of government and resistance to changes in the established social order. Most conservative political parties are right-wing, but some countries do have conservative political parties that are left-wing. All conservatives place a high value on tradition, which refers to standards and institutions that have been demonstrated to foster good. Conservatives view traditional values as authoritative, and judge the world by the standards they have come to believe in, including a belief in God. Conservatives consider tradition to be above the political process. They also disagree with the laws and constitutions of liberal democracies that allow behavior that is in opposition to traditional values. Conservatives in a democracy opt to participate, separate, or resist. Participation on the part of conservatives in a democracy usually takes the form of liberal republican politics, in which conservatives use government policy to promote their values. The imposition of conservative values on the public is typical of nationalist or religious conservatives.

Green politics

Green politics is a political ideology based on environmentalism and sustainability. It is seen as an alternative to both left and right-wing views, and individuals identifying themselves with the left or right tend to view green politics as distinct from their own ideology. As a movement, green politics typically grows at a slow rate but does not readily lose support to other views or parties over time. Some of the features of green politics include support of consensus decision making, participatory democracy and deliberative democracy; green taxes; alternative measures of economic growth;

opposition to the subsidy of pollution by government; opposition to nuclear power, persistent organic pollutants, and biological forms of pollution; investing in human capital; accounting reform; an end to the War on Drugs in the United States and Europe; an end to the War on Terrorism and the curtailment of civil rights.

Pacifism

Pacifism is an ideology that is based on opposition to war. Pacifism varies from a preference for the use of non-military means in resolving disputes to complete opposition to the use of violence or force in any situation. Pacifism may be based on principle or pragmatism. Pacifism based on principle is founded on the belief that war, violence, force and coercion are morally wrong. Pacifism based on pragmatism is founded on the belief that there are preferable means of resolving disputes than war, and that the costs of war outweigh the benefits. An individual who opposes war is often referred to as a dove or dovish, alluding to the peaceful nature of the dove.

Republicanism

Republicanism is a political ideology founded on the concept of a nation being governed by an elected representative rather than a monarch. Today, the elected representative is most often referred to as the President. A republic is a state in which sovereignty resides with the people, as well as a political system in which individual liberty is protected through the power of citizens to elect representatives. These representatives are responsible to the citizens who elected them and govern according to law. Republicanism also represents the ideologies of the political parties that identify themselves as the Republican Party.

Independent country

An independent country shares four defining characteristics:
Any independent country inhabits a specific territory (land and water) defined by boundaries. The sizes and shapes of countries differ widely.
Each country has a population that occupies its territory. The sizes and constitutions of each country are also extremely variable.
Any independent country possesses sovereignty, which is the freedom to control and protect its territory, population, and foreign interactions without outside influence. The geographic location and landscape of a country's territory may affect its ability to defend its sovereignty. For example, the high mountains surrounding Switzerland have served to protect the country against foreign invasion for centuries.
Every independent country has a government, an institution that creates and enforces laws and policies and acts to further the public good (through protection, the maintenance of order, and provision of certain services). There are several types of government structures and governmental authority.

Government structures

Governments may be classified by the nature of the relationship between the central governing body and the smaller units (states, provinces, etc.) that make up a country. Three types of government structures include the following:
- A unitary system exists when a central governmental body exerts sole control over an entire country. The principle government formulates policies applicable at all levels of government; smaller units exert power only if the central government grants it to them.

- 96 -

- A federation exists when certain powers are allocated to a central government and certain powers are given to regional or local governmental units. In a federation (such as the United States), <u>federal, state, and local governments share political power.</u>
- A confederation exists when smaller governmental units retain their sovereignties and allow the central government only specific, limited powers (usually regarding national defense or international trade). In this type of structure, states and provinces retain a large degree of independence but still ally to address common concerns.

Anarchies, democracies, and oligarchies

A government may be classified by the source of its authority. Different kinds of governments are run with various degrees of public participation. In an anarchy, every citizen in the population is seen as a qualified participant in decision-making which will affect the country. There is no central governing body—people govern themselves. A democracy also involves rule by the people. However, unlike an anarchy, a democracy includes a central government that aims to serve the people. In a representative democracy, citizens exercise their political franchise or suffrage (the right to vote) in the selection of leaders, who, in turn, participate in governmental proceedings and make political decisions. Citizens of a democratic nation also express their opinions about certain issues by voting. In an oligarchy, political power is concentrated in the hands of a small group, usually made up of wealthy people with strong military influence and/or familial traditions of power. Often, the most influential participants in an oligarchic government operate outside the public eye in the economic realm.

Representative democracy

In a system of government characterized as a representative democracy, voters elect representatives to act in their interests. Typically, a representative is elected by and responsible to a specific subset of the total population of eligible voters; this subset of the electorate is referred to as a representative's constituency. Countries that function as representative democracies set clear, explicit limits on what elected officials can do. Traits that are consistent among all representative democracies include open elections, the force acceptance of majority decisions, and a one person/ one vote policy. A representative democracy may foster a more powerful legislature than other forms of government systems; to compensate for a strong legislature, most constitutions stipulate that measures must be taken to balance the powers within government, such as the creation of a separate judicial branch. In a representative democracy, power is given to the office, not to the holder of the office. Dissent and criticism of elected officials is not only tolerated in such as system, it is considered necessary to maintain effectiveness. The challenge of the representative democracy is to make sure that all groups in a society feel that they have a chance to express their views, and that minority groups are not trampled by the will of the majority. Representative democracy became popular in post-industrial nations where increasing numbers of people expressed an interest in politics, but where technology and census counts remained incompatible with systems of direct democracy. Today, the majority of the world's population resides in representative democracies, including constitutional monarchies that possess a strong representative branch.

Democracy

Democracy, or rule by the people, is a form of government in which power is vested in the people and in which policy decisions are made by the majority in a decision-making process such as an election that is open to all or most citizens. Definitions of democracy have become more generalized and include aspects of society and political culture in democratic societies that do not necessarily represent a form of government. What defines a democracy varies, but some of the characteristics of a democracy could include the presence of a middle class, the presence of a civil society, a free market, political pluralism, universal suffrage, and specific rights and freedoms. In practice however, democracies do have limits on specific freedoms, which are justified as being necessary to maintain democracy and ensure democratic freedoms. For example, freedom of association is limited in democracies for individuals and groups that pose a threat to government or to society.

Anarchism

Anarchism is a philosophy that is synonymous with anti-authoritarianism. Many people wrongly associate anarchism with chaos, but in fact anarchists embrace political philosophies and social movements that support the abolition of government and social hierarchy. In a system that is based on anarchism, political and economic institutions would not exist. Rather, individual and community relationships would be voluntary, and people would strive towards a society based on autonomy and freedom. On the one hand, anarchists oppose coercive institutions and social hierarchies, and on the other they advocate a positive conception of how a voluntary society could work. As with many political ideologies, there are many factions that fall under the umbrella of anarchism that hold varying opinions of how anarchism should be defined. For instance, some anarchists support the use of violence to promote their ideology, while others do not.

Oligarchy

Oligarchy, or rule by the few, is a form of political system in which the majority of political power is held by a small portion of society. This power usually resides with the most powerful individuals or groups, such as those that possess wealth, military might, or political influence. Oftentimes, oligarchies are comprised of a few powerful families, in which power is passed on from one generation to the next. Members of oligarchies may not wield their power openly, but may instead exercise power from behind the scenes, particularly through economic measures.

Aristocracy, meritocracy, and plutocracy

Aristocracy is a form of oligarchic system in which the government is led by a ruling class that is considered, either by themselves or by others, to be superior to other members of society. Meritocracy, or rule by those who most deserve to rule, is a system that is more flexible than an aristocracy. In a meritocracy, rulers are not automatically considered the best rulers for life, but must demonstrate their abilities and achievements in order to maintain power. A plutocracy is a system of government led by the wealthy. There is often an overlap between the classification of a government as an aristocracy and a plutocracy, because wealth can enable individuals to portray their own qualities and merits as the best.

Authoritarianism

Authoritarian regimes enforce strong, even oppressive, measures against individuals that fall within their sphere of influence; they often arise when a governing body presumes that it knows what is right for a nation and enforces it. They are typically led by an elite group that employs repressive measures to maintain power, and they do not generally make efforts to gain the consent of individuals or permit feedback on their policies. Under an authoritarian government, people are often subject to government control over aspects of their lives that in many other systems would be considered personal matters. There is a spectrum of authoritarian ideologies. Examples of authoritarian regimes include absolute monarchies and dictatorships. Democracies can also exhibit authoritarian characteristics in some situations, such as efforts to promote national security. Authoritarian governments typically extend broad-reaching powers to law enforcement bodies, sometimes resulting in a police state. They may or may not have a rule of law, and are often corrupt.

Until fairly recently, most countries across the world had authoritarian governments. Today, various forms of democracy are more common. There are different degrees of authoritarianism:
- A monarchy is a type of authoritarian government in which monarchs (for example, queens, shahs, and pharaohs) inherit political power simply by being born into a ruling family. Monarchs may serve as symbols of national unity, or they may rule as dictators.
- A dictatorship (the most common type of authoritarian government) is a system in which political power is held by a small group or even a unitary individual. The dictator(s) exert control through military force and intimidation and they attempt to control the behavior of their subordinates.
- Totalitarianism is the most extreme form of authoritarianism. In this kind of system, the ruling body tries to control every aspect of society in its territory, from economic activity to people's personal lives.

Monarchy

Monarchy, or rule by a single individual, is one of the oldest forms of government and is defined as an autocratic system in which a monarch serves as Head of State. In such a system, the monarch holds office for life. Also included in a monarchy are the individuals and institutions that comprise the royal establishment. In elective monarchies, monarchs are appointed to their position for life; in most instances, elective monarchies been succeeded by hereditary monarchies. In a hereditary monarchy, the title of monarch is inherited according to a line of succession; typically one family can trace its origin along a dynasty or bloodline. Most monarchs represent merely a symbol of continuity and statehood, rather than actually serving as a participant in partisan politics. The practice of choosing a monarch varies between countries. A constitutional monarchy is one in which the rule of succession is typically established by a law passed by a representative body.

Totalitarianism

Totalitarianism is a form of authoritarian political system in which the government regulates practically every aspect of public and private conduct. Under totalitarianism, individuals and institutions are enveloped into the state's ideology, and the government imposes its political authority by exercising absolute and centralized control over all aspects of life. Totalitarian regimes typically have an ideology that encompasses all parts of social life, and some kind of organization (or political party) for maintaining control. Individuals are subordinate to the state, and opposition to political and cultural expression is suppressed. Totalitarian regimes do not tolerate activities by individuals or groups that are not geared toward achieving the state's goals and maintaining the state's ideology. A totalitarian regime maintains power via the use of secret police, propaganda disseminated through government controlled media, regulation and restriction of free speech, and use of terror tactics. This organization is led by a dictator, who demands total subservience from his citizens. For a long time, scholars assumed that the Nazi and Soviet states functioned in this way, though later research has uncovered a host of inefficiencies and internal debate. Totalitarian regimes generally emerge from states of chaos, in which a confused and disoriented public will embrace any coherent ideology.

Police state

A police state is a form of a totalitarian political system. A nation does not identify itself as a police state; rather, the characterization is applied by critics of the nation. A police state is regulated by police, who exercise power on behalf of an executive authority. It is very difficult to challenge the police and question their conduct in a police state, and there is no rule of law; the law is simply the will of the leader. The police state is based on the concept of enlightened despotism, under which the leader exercises absolute power with the goal of providing for the good of a nation; opposition to government policy is an offense against authority, and therefore against the nation itself. Because public dissent is not allowed, people who oppose the government must do so in secret. Therefore, the police must resort to the use of informers and secret police to seek out dissenters.

Autocracy, absolutism, despotism, dictatorship

Autocracy is a form of a political system in which unlimited power is held by a single person. Absolutism is a form of autocratic political system. Absolutists believe that one person should hold all power. Historically, a monarch ruled in a system characterized as absolutist. Some people believed that an absolute ruler was chosen by God; in this case opposition against the monarch was equivalent to opposition to God. Therefore, rule was considered absolute in the sense that the ruler could not be challenged. Despotism is another form of autocratic political system, characterized as having a government overseen by a single authority that wields absolute power; the authority could be either an individual or a group. A dictatorship is a form of absolute rule by a leader, referred to as a dictator, who is unrestricted by law, constitutions, or other social and political forces. Dictatorships are typically associated with single-party states, military regimes, and other forms of authoritarianism.

Patriarchy and tyranny

A patriarchy is a form of autocratic system in which the male members of society tend to hold positions of power. In such a system, the more powerful a position is, the more likely it is that a male will hold that position. Patriarchy also describes systems that are characterized as having male leadership in certain hierarchical churches or religious bodies. Tyranny is also a form of autocratic system, in which an individual described as a tyrant possesses and wields absolute power and rules by tyranny. Tyrants are typically characterized as cruel despots that place greater significance on their own interests or the interests of a small group of individuals than on the interests of the population and the state that they govern.

Parliamentary system

A parliamentary system is a representative democratic system in which the executive branch of government is dependent on the support of a parliament. In this system, there is no obvious separation of powers between the executive and legislative branches. However, parliamentary systems are generally flexible and responsive to the public. They are characterized as having both a head of government, who is typically the prime minister, and a head of state, who is often a symbol possessing only ceremonial powers. Some parliamentary systems also have an elected president. The features of a parliamentary system include an executive cabinet, headed by the head of government. The cabinet can be removed by the parliament by a vote of no confidence, and likewise the parliament can be dissolved by the executive.

Presidential/congressional system

In a presidential system, also referred to as a congressional system, the legislative branch and the executive branches are elected separately from one another. The features of a presidential system include a president who serves as both the head of state and the head of the government, who has no formal relationship with the legislative branch, who is not a voting member, who cannot introduce bills, and who has a fixed term of office. Elections are held at scheduled times. The president's cabinet carries out the policies of the executive branch and the legislative branch.

Communism

Communism is a form of an authoritarian, or in some cases totalitarian, political system. A communist country is governed by a single political party that upholds the principles of Marxism-Leninism. The goal of communism is to dissolve the state into a classless society. According to Marxism, a communist state is one in which the resources and means of production are communally owned rather than individually owned and which provides for equal sharing of all freedoms, work and benefits. According to Marx, this state would occur when the proletariat, or working class, overthrew their bourgeois masters. In a communist state, property is owned by the community and capital is divided equitably. Communism is distinguished from socialism in that it arises after a revolution, rather than as the crowning phase of a long social transition. Marxism argues that socialism is a necessary intermediate phase in achieving communism. Therefore, states that are governed by a communist party are actually socialist states, and not true communist states, since a true communist state could not exist given the goal of elimination of the state. Historically, communist states have often arisen during political instability. Within communist states there have rarely been restrictions on state power, resulting in state structures which are totalitarian or authoritarian. Marxist-Leninist ideology views any restriction on state power as an interference in the goal of reaching communism. The communism that appeared in the Soviet Union after the Russian Revolution of 1917 never fully realized the spirit of Marx, since a massive and greedy bureaucracy controlled production and distributed benefits unfairly. Most states that still purport to be communist (for instance China and Cuba) are gradually moving towards a more free market approach.

Socialism

Socialism is a political system that attempts to eliminate the vicious competitiveness of capitalism, in favor of a social structure based on cooperation and equality. Socialists seek to establish an economy that works for the good of all members of the society, not just the members of a privileged class. Typically, is accomplished by taking the control over the means of production from the bourgeoisie and returning it to the workers (proletariat) themselves. Socialism in practice has had mixed results: although some of the socialist reforms in Western Europe, for instance the nationalization of some industries, have been successes, the full-scale implementation of socialism in the Soviet Union and other Eastern European countries never realized the visions of its architects.

Socialist republic

In a socialist republic, the constitution or other political doctrine stipulates that the republic operates under a socialist economic system, such as a Marxist system. Some socialist republics are under the power of a party whose platform is founded on communist ideology, and as such are referred to as communist states by Western nations.

Examples of republics that use the term socialist in their names include the Democratic Socialist Republic of Sri Lanka and the former Socialist Federal Republic of Yugoslavia. Some countries that define themselves as socialist republics, such as India and Guyana, do so in their constitutions rather than in their names. Other countries that identify themselves as socialist republics include North Korea, the People's Republic of China, and Cuba.

Fascism

Fascism is an authoritarian political ideology and defined the form of rule in Italy from 1922 to 1943 under the leadership under Mussolini. Fascism is characterized by efforts to exert state control over all aspects of life, to hold the nation and political party above the individual, and to hold the state as supreme. Fascism also emphasizes loyalty to a single leader, and submission to a single nationalistic culture. Fascists support corporatism as an economic system, in which economic and social interests of diverse individuals are combined with the interests of the state.

Nazism

Nazism was the ideology of the National Socialist German Workers Party which was led by Adolf Hitler in Nazi Germany from 1933 to 1945, during the Third Reich. Followers of Nazism believed that the Aryan race was superior to other races, and promoted Germanic racial supremacy and a strong, centrally governed state. Nazism is illegal in modern Germany, but small factions of Neo-Nazis continue to exist both in Germany and abroad. Nazis believed that military power would produce a strong nation, opposed multilingualism and multiculturalism, and sought the unification of all German-speaking individuals. Qualities of Nazism included racism, anti-Semitism, the desire for the creation of a master race, anti-Slavism, the belief in the superiority of the White, Germanic, Aryan or Nordic races, anti-Marxism, anti-Communism, and anti-Bolshevism, rejection of democracy, social Darwinism, eugenics, environmental protection, rejection of the modern art movement and an embrace of classical art, and defense of the Nazi flag.

Republic

A republic is a state in which supreme power rests with citizens who vote to elect representatives to be responsible to them. The organization of government in a republic can vary. In most republics the head of state is referred to as the President, and in a democratic republic the head of state is chosen in an election. In some countries the constitution restricts the number of terms that an individual can serve as president. In the United States, where the head of state is also the head of government, the system is known as a presidential system.

Federal republic

A federal republic is a state that defines itself as both a federation and a republic. A federation is a state that is made up of multiple self-governing regions that are united by a central, federal government. The self-government of independent states is guaranteed by a constitution and is not able to be repealed by the central government. There are three countries that currently characterize themselves as federal republics. These three countries are the Federal Republic of Germany, the Federal Republic of Nigeria, and the Federal Democratic Republic of Ethiopia.

Commonwealth

A commonwealth is a state that is founded on law and that is united by a compact or by an agreement made by its citizens for the common good of the entire state and for the citizens of the state. In a commonwealth, supreme authority is held by the people. In the United States, the state of Kentucky, the state of Massachusetts, the state of Pennsylvania, and the state of Virginia are all classified as commonwealths. The term commonwealth is also used to describe Puerto Rico and the Northern Marianas Islands, which are both self-governing, autonomous political units that voluntarily associate themselves with the United States of America.

Theocracy

A theocracy is a form of a government system in which religion or faith plays a significant role in the way that the government is run. Commonly, in countries that identify themselves as a theocracy, civil rulers are also the leaders of the dominant religion. In these countries, government policies are often strongly guided by religion. Usually, a theocratic government makes a claim to rule on behalf of God or another higher power. The administrative hierarchy of the government often serves as the administrative hierarchy of the dominant religion as well.

Tribalism

Tribalism was the first social system that humans created and coexisted in. It is a system in which society is divided into relatively independent groups referred to as tribes. In such a society, tribes themselves have some level of organizational structure, but there is generally very little organization between tribes. Tribes are typically characterized by simple internal organization and structure, with very few differences in social status between individuals. Some tribes nurture the belief that all individuals are equal, and many tribes do not embrace the concept of private property.

Economics

The study of economics includes microeconomics, which is concerned with smaller units, such as individuals and firms, and macroeconomics, which looks at the economy as a composite, taking a more global view. In general, economics deals with topics such as scarcity, supply, demand, and choices made by various parts of the economy and the total economy. There are a variety of economic topics that overlap both microeconomics and macroeconomics. These hybrid areas may be covered separately or as a part of the micro/macroeconomic spectrum. Now called "mainstream" economics is blend of macroeconomics and economic theory developed in the last 50 years. This includes a number of schools of economic thought, each with its own assumptions, conclusions, and methodology. Economics centers on the idea of scarce resources and how to best utilize these resources to meet the needs of individuals and the economic system as a whole.

Modern economics

Modern economics is based on one basic premise - that resources are scarce and limited, and that choices must be made in the acquisition and use of them. All other questions and alternatives flow from this assumption. Economic choices involve sacrificing something in order to obtain another thing. This sacrifice is called the 'opportunity cost" of the choice. I may choose to spend my last dollar on a candy bar rather than a writing tablet - thus the opportunity cost of the candy bar is the tablet. There are seemingly endless choices in a consumer society, all of which involve choices and opportunity costs. The choices and opportunity costs are expressed in price relationships in modern economics. Each individual makes many economic decisions (choices) each day and the aggregate reflects economic activity of a society. Choices are driven by the utility, or want-satisfying abilities of the goods and services. Choices are ranked on the ability of the good or service to fill a perceived need of the individual. This utility function is active in most, but not all, economic choices.

Microeconomic theory

The development of economic theory as it relates to individual units in a society is called microeconomics. These units may be individuals, firms, labor forces, resource pools, and consumers. The behavior of both people and businesses is included in microeconomics. The term itself means "small scale" economics. Microeconomics questions how the activities of small units in an economy interact, and the implications of such transactions. The utilization of scarce resources by individuals and firms is a central topic in microeconomics. Models of the marketplace where households and commercial companies interact and trade are key components in microeconomics. Economic activity is sometimes viewed as a process between corporations, businesses, and individuals. This process illustrates the mechanisms of a market economy when studied from small individual
units within that economy. Relationships between scarce assets, such as natural resources, money, labor, and the factors of production are all easily visualized from the individual level of economics.

Microeconomics and macroeconomics

While microeconomics studies the individual units of economic activity, macroeconomics takes a larger view. It is the analysis of the aggregate of all the economic actions of individuals, corporations and businesses. This expanded scope includes the issues of government policies to influence the economy. Such national goals include suppressing inflation, stimulating the economy through monetary and fiscal policy, and attaining a maximum employment level. The conduct and regulation of international trade is another area of national interest.
There are a multiple number of economic schools of thought that influence macroeconomics. Macroeconomics is an area of continuing evolution, and various tools of economic analysis are used from a variety of sources. The goal of all such schools is to provide the most current and precise economic data and analysis available. Research carried out by different patterns of economic thinking are combined to produce the most useful and accurate information.

Analytical approaches
The two broad divisions of economic analysis are Keynesians theory, developed in the 20th century by the English economist, John Maynard Keynes, and supply side economics, a current favorite of more conservative economists. Keynesian economics proposes government action to stimulate demand in an economy. Supply side economics is concerned with the policies that will encourage increased supply by manufacturers and other business organizations. Keynes believed that aggregate demand was the key to understanding fluctuations in the economy. He argued for strong government interventions to attain these goals. Much of the New Deal economics applied during the depression of the 1930's was based on Keynes theories. The so called "supply-siders" emphasizes the role of the aggregate money supply and fiscal action (or inaction) as the crucial factors in economic growth.

Political economics

Political economics is an umbrella term that includes a wide variety of economic approaches to study and predict behavior. It often uses techniques and tools from other social sciences in its applications. Political economy is a maverick in economic theory, as it often contravenes accepted economic doctrine. Interdisciplinary by definition, political economy studies the interactions of social and political factors on economic issues that affect markets. The term originally was used in political science to compare and contrast relationships of geopolitics between countries. A number of political-social-economic schools have made political economy their main interest. The historical long term implications of political economy are of great interest to economic historians.

The Market

The central arena of political economy is the marketplace where economic activity occurs. It is also the intersecting point of the sometimes competing economic interests and forces at play. Common causes may be found by unlikely allies and groups may be pitted against each other for economic advantage.
In a capitalistic economic system, the major task of the state is the creation and preservation of capital and the economic choices involved in its allocation.
Socialism maintains that decisions and implementation of production should be determined by the power of the state, ostensibly to create the greatest good for the most people. This philosophy brings socialism into conflict with capitalism that requires that fundamental economic power should be in private hands. Communism seeks control over all factors of production as well as political and social dominance over its society.

Economic system

An economic system addresses the production, distribution and consumption of goods and services within society and focuses on solving the economic problems of the allocation and scarcity of resources. The composition of an economic system consists of people and institutions, and the relationships between them. The three questions that must be answered in an economic system are 1) what to produce, 2) how to produce it, and 3) for whom to produce. There are many different types of economic systems, which are often associated with particular ideologies and political systems. Examples of economic systems include market economies, mixed economies, planned economies, traditional economies, and participatory economies.

Capitalism

Capitalism is an economic system in which the means of production are privately owned, in which the investment of capital, and the production, distribution and prices of goods and services are determined in a free market, and in which the goal of production is to generate profits. The features of a capitalist economic system include a private sector, private property, free enterprise, and profit. Other features of a capitalist economic system include unequal distribution of wealth, competition, self-organization, the existence of markets, the existence of both a bourgeoisie class and a proletariat class, and the pursuit of self-interest. In theory, capitalism allows any citizen to benefit him or herself by increasing efficiency. Typically, the means of production are owned almost entirely by private interests, and operated for the profit of the owners. The role of the government is simply to protect property rights and make sure that trade is conducted fairly. Some proponents of capitalism, however, claim that any government interference is damaging to the market, and that for this reason there has never been an instance of pure capitalism. Sociologists and economists are split as to whether capitalist economies tend to enrich or impoverish more people.

Feudalism

Feudalism is a political and economic system that was in existence in Europe from the ninth century through the fifteenth century. Feudalism in the Medieval Age was based on the relationships between lords and vassals and fiefs. A lord was a person who held a title of nobility and who owned land. A vassal was an individual who was loaned a piece of land by a lord. The piece of land that was owned by the lord and loaned to the vassal was referred to as a fief. In exchange for being loaned the fief, the vassal provided military service to the lord.

Socialism

Socialism referrers to an economic system in which the means of production and the distribution of goods and services are owned collectively or are owned by a centralized government that often plans and controls the economy. In practice, socialism also refers to the economic phase in Marxist-Leninist theory that falls somewhere between capitalism and communism, in which collective ownership of the economy by the proletariat, or the working class, has not yet been achieved. The goal of a socialist economic system is to achieve collective ownership and, ultimately, to achieve a classless society.

Mixed economy

A mixed economy is an economic system blending capitalism and socialism. Such a system is characterized by both private economic freedom and by centralized economic planning. The majority of Western countries, including the United States, have a mixed economy. Features of a mixed economy include the freedoms to possess means of production, to travel, to buy and sell, to hire and fire, to organize labor unions or associations, the freedom of communication, and the freedom to protest peacefully. In addition, mixed economies typically provide legal assistance, libraries, roads, schools, hospitals, protection of person and property both at home and abroad, subsidies to agriculture and other businesses, and government monopolies and government-granted monopolies, all of which are funded by taxes or subsidies. There are provisions for autonomy over personal finances, but mixed economies also include socially-oriented involuntary spending programs such as welfare, social security, and government subsidies for businesses. Mixed economies also impose environmental, labor, consumer, antitrust, intellectual property, corporate, and import and export laws, as well as taxes and fees.

Colonialism and imperialism

Colonialism is a political and economic system that is defined as the extension of a nation's sovereignty over territory and people outside its own boundaries, often amounting to the exploitation of a weaker country by a relatively stronger country. Most often the stronger country is interested in the use of the weaker country's resources, including labor, to strengthen and enrich itself. Colonialism also refers to the set of beliefs and values that is used to validate and advance this system, particularly the belief that the culture and civilization of the relatively stronger colonizing country are superior to those of the relatively weaker colonized country. Imperialism is a policy of extending control or authority over foreign countries via territorial acquisition or by the establishment of economic and political control over other countries.

Neo-colonialism

Neocolonialism is a political and economic system in which a powerful country uses economic and political measures to extend, or to continue, its influence over less developed countries. The term was devised to describe circumstances at the international level after the fall of European colonial empires in the nineteenth and twentieth centuries, particularly the phenomenon of countries and multinational corporations seeking control over other countries through indirect means, such as economic policies, as opposed to the direct military-political control that traditional colonial powers sought. Many people argue that economic tools, such as restrictions on trade and embargos, that are employed by stronger, more developed countries in their relations with less developed countries are reminiscent of colonial power.

Command/Planned economy

A planned economy is an economic system in which decisions about the production, allocation and consumption of goods and services is planned in advance; planning can be carried out in either a centralized or decentralized approach. In most planned economies, the plans are carried out by means of commands; therefore planned economies are also commonly referred to as command economies. An economic system that is centrally-planned by a government is generally referred to as economic statism. Economic statism, by definition, is the practice of giving a centralized government control over economic planning and policy.

Laissez-faire economics

The concept of laissez-faire economics is associated with capitalist economic systems and is synonymous with strict free market economics. Proponents of laissez-faire economics oppose government regulation of or interference in the economy beyond the minimum measures that are necessary to ensure that a free market system can operate according to its own economic laws. Proponents hold the opinion that the free market can and should operate in the absence of government interference, as the market itself will purge inefficiencies in a more competent and timely manner than government could. The premise of laissez-faire economics is that less government involvement in economic decisions such as pricing, production, and distribution of goods and services will foster a healthier, stronger and more efficient economy.

Economic interdependence

Economic interdependence is a situation in which two or more countries depend on one other for any or all of the following: energy, food, manufactured goods, minerals, or labor. Resources (including natural resources such as minerals and land as well as human resources), fuel sources, and information are distributed unevenly across the globe—no single country possesses all the resources it needs to subsist and thrive. Therefore, each must trade its surplus goods and services for those it lacks. The North American Free Trade Agreement (NAFTA) was formed among three economically interdependent countries (Canada, the United States, and Mexico) in an attempt to ease trade restrictions on vital imports and exports in the member states.

Levels of development

Economic geographers use different terms to classify countries by their levels of economic development:
- Most broadly, countries may be classified as either more developed countries (MDCs) or less developed countries (LDCs). In this system of classification, distinctions are often made based on political factors as well as economic factors.
- Geographers may also categorize the level of a country's economic development as First World (capitalist), Second World (communist or socialist), Third World (underdeveloped), Fourth World (severely underdeveloped), or Fifth World (poorest).
- Currently, the World Bank (an international organization that monitors the economic status of countries) classifies countries as high income, upper-middle income, lower-middle income, or low income.

Any of these categorizations may be misleading when applied to an entire country. Most of the world's countries exhibit highly-developed cores as well as peripheral regions stricken by poverty. Therefore, averages of national economic statistics have lost some of their meaning. It is useful to consider the relative advantages (geographic location, resources, political stability, etc) of certain countries over others.

Underdevelopment

Third World countries that do not have the modern economic conditions possessed by the wealthier nations are said to suffer from underdevelopment. That is, they do not have the industrial, social, or political strength that is requires being a self-sustaining party in the global economy. In some countries, underdevelopment is clearly the result of dysfunctional politics: Third World nations are more likely to be ruled by a small group or by a dictator. Underdeveloped nations are typically those that were colonized at one time. Because their economy during the colonial period was so heavily based on exporting raw materials, they never created a manufacturing base and found themselves unequipped for independence. Sociologists are at odds as to whether First World nations should aid underdeveloped countries by funneling money to them, or by helping them to develop modern economies.

Developmental economics

Developing countries have unique economic problems that more sophisticate economies do not. Particularly important is the area of long term economic growth in developing economies. This field is called developmental economics. It also includes the microeconomic analyses of individuals and firms in such fledgling economies. A highly analytical field that uses econometrics (mathematical applications to economics) to predict economic patterns. Usually both mathematical and qualitative tools are used to measure and predict economic activity in developing countries. Included in the field is the problem of long term debt, and the action of international economic agencies such as the International Monetary Fund. The problem of encouraging and sustaining economic growth in such countries is a primary objective of economists. The field includes not only economic issues and tools, but also social and political methods to influence the whole society.

Modernization

Modernization is the process by which societies develop sophisticated industrial technology, as well as the political, cultural, and social systems that are most effective in sustaining, and advancing that technology. For a long time, sociologists noted that the most modernized countries, namely the Western empires, were the most successful, and that other societies should strive to emulate them. In recent decades, however, more sensitive sociologists have declared that modernization need not be equated with Westernization, and that the indigenous cultures of South America and Africa, for example, need not be cast off for these places to enjoy prosperity. One way sociologists can assess the relative modernization of a society is by comparing the gross national product: the total value of all economic activity within a society. Often, GNP is divided by total population to determine a society's per capita gross national product.

<u>Theories</u>
The state theory of modernization supports the ideals of capitalism by maintaining that whenever the government is restricted from seizing private property, capitalism will develop and free markets will arise, as people modernize and strive to become more productive. The world system theory of modernization, also known as the dependency theory, states that some nations modernize at the expense of less-developed nations, and that so long as this exploitation continues, the less-developed nations will be unable to improve their lot. This theory essentially takes the Marxist view of the capitalist society, in which those who own the means of production are able to maintain dominance over the workers, and applies it to the interactions of nations.

Finance

The use of money as an economic resource, including the individual and business decisions regarding the obtaining, utilization, and allocation of financial resources after evaluating risk potential. Thus finance studies the uses of money and comparable assets, and the effective management of these assets, risk appraisal and the provision of funds for business operations. Finance is also defined as the collective policies and operations that business entities (or individuals) manage their business activities. Primary aspects of these operations include management of income and costs, and alternatives in investment choices.
These choices are determined by management decisions as how best to utilize excess income. Excess income may be invested, loaned to borrowers, or reinvested in the business to improve operations. These economic decisions are important to the growth and economic health of the entity.

Money

Money has been defined as any store of value which has intrinsic value or is a representation of a store of value (bank notes). Money is the lifeblood of market transactions, serving as a measure of value, a medium of exchange, and as an accounting convention. As a means to exchange value for goods and services money has no peer. But for this to be the case, money must have a guaranteed and obvious value of its own. Historically, commodities including crops and livestock were the first forms of money. When money became accepted as a representation of commodities, the market system was revolutionized. It made simple trading and quickly became an accepted medium of exchange. In earlier times, money represented the commodities of precious metals, notably gold and silver. In modern economies, money depends on the guarantee of the government to honor its value. These guarantees permit international trade without risk about the value of the money involved.

<u>Qualities</u>
All money or forms of exchange share common characteristics which define the store of value of the currency used. Money must be a generally accepted medium for trading and settling debts. Acceptance of money depends on trust in the issuing institution or nation.
To be useful as a deferred payment instrument, money must serve as a basic unit of account in an economic system. This requisite is fulfilled if money is seen to be a standard of value through which other goods may be given comparative value. The relative cost of any good or service must be measured against a standard which is the value of money. Perhaps most importantly, money must be accepted a store of value by everyone in an economy. In this manner money is a representation of the essential worth of any traded good or service. The system of deferred payment under which most markets operate make it imperative that money has its own essential store of value resting on the promise of a central bank or nation to honor the currency.

<u>History of forms of money</u>
The first "money" was commodities that were traded under a barter system. The next advance in the form of money was the minting of coins of precious metals, usually silver and gold. This form of money had intrinsic value but was a very limited resource. It could be transported fairly easily in moderate amounts, and was difficult to forge. The next leap in the form of money was the advent of paper notes, issued and guaranteed by governments. In modern economies money has taken on a variety of new forms, some a result of increasing technological advances. Modern economies feature paper notes backed by the central bank and government who issues them. Coins with a small percentage of silver or gold are also assets honored by central banks. The intrinsic value of precious metals in most coins is negligible. By far the most revolutionary change in the form of money has occurred in the last 100 years. Demand deposits, credit cards, commercial paper, certificates of deposit, mortgages, and public and private promissory notes are all a form of money today.

Monetary system

As in other markets, the same elements of analysis may be used for the money market. The laws of demand and supply apply to the money market and result in market equilibrium for the price of money. The quantity of money in the system is also a product of these forces.
Money in circulation includes actual paper money and coins. Paper money may be banknotes or Federal Reserve notes that are physically produced by the United State's mint but represent money created by the Federal Reserve based on the credit of the federal government. This credit is electronically created by the government to influence the economy. In reality, since all paper money is based on the promise of the government to honor the currency, all notes are electronically produced. Coins may be produced outside of the Federal Reserve system by legislation. The total money supply is within the scope of the Federal Reserve system.

Gold standard

A monetary system linked to the value of gold is said to be on the gold standard. Those who issue currency agree to exchange bank notes and coins for gold based on a fixed exchange rate. Thus gold becomes the basic unit of account to measure all wealth against. Gold standards were originally created to stabilize currencies by making it impossible for governments to create money at their pleasure. The gold standard also protects against hyper-inflation and the over -expansion of debt in an economy. Originally, when the major form of money was coins (usually silver or gold) there was a logic to the gold standard.

The gold standard was once a common phenomenon among nations, but has now been replaced by systems giving the central banks of countries the power to create money and manipulate monetary policy for the good of the economy. No modern country would return to the gold standard despite the protection it affords.

Historical use of gold

Gold was historically considered to be the ideal measure of wealth and a practical unit of account for market transactions. Gold was rare, easily measured and divided (originally by weight), extremely durable, and provided a uniform measure of value that transcended geographical boundaries making it ideal for settling debts between nations or individuals living in different areas. Gold may be easily transported and was used as a convenient base for the early banking systems in the world. Bank notes and other forms of paper currencies have obvious practical advantages over gold. Besides providing central banks with the power to create money, paper currencies are portable, resistant to hoarding, and may now be transferred electronically for speed and simplicity. The complexity of the world economy made gold obsolete in the modern world except as an investment or reserve. International trade in the modern world could not be conducted with gold as the measure of value.

The World Bank

The World Bank was chartered in 1944 when the post World War II devastation of economies was a major global concern.
The organization addressed the problems of rebuilding the economies of Western Europe and provided stability for international investment in those countries (as well as other developing nations). In recent decades, the World Bank has become an active participant in reducing poverty and promoting economic growth in third world countries. Included in the economic support is the improvement of education, farming, and manufacturing technology.
The major financial tool of the World Bank is to provide funds through loans to these countries. The loans usually carry a much lower interest rate than what normally would be charged. The World Bank is actually an association of five separate but related agencies working toward a common goal. It is highly regarded as an organization of integrity by economists and governments alike.

Production

The production function in microeconomics refers to the total process of producing or assembling goods and services that are to be traded in a marketplace. Production decisions are some of the most vital in microeconomics. A firm or individual must decide what to make, and how many units to provide. This will often depend on the method of production and the unit price of making each product. An evaluation on the necessary resources to be utilized is another important production decision. In tandem with sophisticated market research, optimum decisions can be made about producing goods and services.
Production is a process, and as such it occurs through time and space. Because it is a flow concept, an important statistic is the amount of production for a specific period of time. Other factors of concern are the amount and physical dimensions of the finished process. This will be important in storing and shipping the finished goods.

Factors of production

Factors of production are the sum total of the resources needed to produce finished goods. The major factors identified by economists include the use of land (for factories and agricultural products), labor, (the human work force), natural resources, (raw materials used in manufacturing), and capital goods, (previously manufactured equipment used in production.) Human inputs such as management and human relations could be added to the mix. Contemporary economists often include technological expertise into the factors of production. Factors of production may be fixed (one which cannot be changed), or variable (one which can be adjusted by management easily). Examples of fixed factors would be physical plants, heavy machinery and key managerial personnel. A variable factor of production is one whose usage rate can be changed easily. In the "long run" all of these factors of production can be adjusted by management. The "short run" however, is defined as a period in which at least one of the factors of production is fixed. These definitions of the factors of production are from classical economics and political economy, and they remain accurate today although the idea of capital has been expanded to include human expertise and technology.

Classical economics identifies three main factors in the production of consumable goods and services:
- Land refers to the physical location at which production occurs, as well as material goods (including natural fuel resources, such as coal, as well as materials such as minerals and soil that are used in production). Rent is the monetary compensation paid for the use of land owned by a separate party.
- Labor refers to the work executed by humans in the production of goods and the performance of services. The quality of labor is affected by education and training levels.
- Capital goods are manmade goods that are used, in turn, to produce other goods and services. Capital goods are also referred to as means of production. This factor includes tools, buildings, and machinery.

Natural resources

A resource is something valued by humans for its role in survival. A natural resource is a naturally-occurring material (such as water, soil, minerals, or animals) that humans use to maintain their existences. Such resources are unevenly distributed across the globe; their monetary values vary with scarcity, technology, and specific human needs. For example, petroleum became much more valuable after the invention of automobiles, which require the substance to operate. Some natural resources are renewable, meaning that they are constantly being replenished in nature. Energy from the sun, water, and soil are all renewable resources. Nonrenewable resources are those of which the Earth has a limited supply. Fossil fuels such as coal and oil take millions of years to form in the Earth's crust; therefore, once humans exhaust the current supply of these resources, no more will become available in our lifetimes. Most natural resources (renewable or nonrenewable) are used to provide energy to fuel modern industry.

Distribution of resources

Resources are not evenly distributed across the globe. Fossil fuels, for example, form over millions of years (under specific natural conditions) from the remains of fossilized plants and animals. Even renewable resources such as water are not equally distributed. Certain global regions experience droughts while others withstand deluges of rain. The uneven distribution of natural resources affects the locations and sizes of human settlements, the quality of life in those settlements, and the economic activities in which certain people can participate. A lack of resources in an area may lead to mass migration to an area with a larger supply or to the formation of trade networks with countries possessing higher quantities of a particular resource.

Capital

Capital is a comprehensive term for all or any methods by which products are made by labor. The more modern concept of capital broadens the definition to include a wide range of assets that are utilized in the production process. This includes a wide variety of tools or elements. Physical capital may include all categories of real objects such as equipment, plants, land, and machinery that contribute to the process of production. Intellectual capital is the necessary ingredient that transforms the production process by human interaction. Included in intellectual capital is the utilization of information, management skills, technological advances, and application of ideas and theories which are catalysts in the economic system. Financial capital represents the operating funds and monetary investment in a business or plant. Financial capital is often obtained by corporations through the issue of stock in exchange for funds. Natural resources such as oceans, forests, mountains, and rivers provide natural capital which may or may not be publicly owned. Capital that is used to provide support systems for fundamental production processes and operating ability is sometimes termed infrastructural capital. Much of this type of capital is represented in plants and equipment. The abilities and acumen gained from education and experience is sometimes referred to as human capital. This incorporates the many types of growth and development from what we call human resources. Although capital is generally regarded as an essential ingredient of benign economic activity, it can also be used to foster the defense of a state or prepare a country for an aggressive war. The designation of large portions of Germany's capital was used to attempt to dominate Europe by the Nazis. Capital is commonly used to further a state's geopolitical aims through peaceful or belligerent goals. The utilization of capital is a prime indicator of any country's goals and ambitions.

Transport, exchange, and infrastructure

Transportation is the network that allows the economy to function. Capital and labor must be moved to land in order to facilitate production. Finished goods must be moved through channels of distribution to be available to consumers. Transport is necessary for the movement of products, people, and capital.
Economic exchange is the basic activity of economics. The circular cycle of exchange from consumer to suppliers and back are the transactions that move an economy. The field of exchange is the marketplace, and money is the medium through which these transactions move. Building an infrastructure for market transactions is necessary to allow an orderly and dependable mechanism for economic exchange.

Consumption

Consumption of goods, services, and ancillary products is the final activity for satisfying the needs and wants of society. When a resource is used and eliminated, it has been consumed. Consumption is an important feature of economics, usually meaning personal consumption of goods and services. Consumption has its own determinants, including economic expectations, level of disposable income, and the propensity to consume. Ultimately consumption is a component of aggregate demand in economic theory. Economics makes a clear distinction between production, the supplying of goods and services, and the consumption, or use of these goods and services. Economic research into consumption raises the questions regarding the motivation and reasons for various levels of consumption. The relatively recent importance of our consumer society has placed this element of economic theory under the microscope of analysis. Consumption in all its forms has developed a significant impact on the lives of everyone in a modern economy. Consumption also may include the less tangible qualities of health, leisure activity, goodwill, and freedom of choice.

Disposal

All excess products of consumption or production must be eliminated as waste. The failure to dispose of these waste products will result in an impaired economy and a degrading of quality of life. Waste removal requires a large physical capacity and the employment of significant capital resources. The increasing urbanization of the world makes waste disposal an important priority. Systems of waste removal include garbage and sewage operations as well as preventative measures of recycling and legislation to protect the environment. Governments must take responsibility for waste removal because of the scope of the problem. The ecological movement and "green" economics of the past 30 years have raised questions on the economics of waste and the quality of life. This has generated increased concern about such issues as destruction of natural habitats, global warming, air and water pollution, and the importance of sustaining our natural resources.

Adaptive expectations

When individuals base their expectations on past economic events and history, it is called "adaptive expectations". An example would be if the stock market has been strong for a period of time, the public will have positive expectations for future advances.
Individuals will base their future economic decisions on the cumulative past experience of recent economic activity. These decisions will become self fulfilling if consumers are pessimistic about the future of the economy. An example of adaptive expectations is the general attitude regarding inflation. In the United States, as well as most of the free world, inflation has become a fact of economic life. The expectation of rising prices, increasing wages, and general cost-of-living increases have bred a culture of inflationary expectation that rarely fails to materialize. Sometimes general pessimism about the economy serves as a deterrent to economic expansion. This is another example of adaptive expectations at work.

GNP

The Gross National Product (GNP) is one of the prime indicators of the economic health of a country. Typically this aggregate figure of all goods and services produced in the economy for a specified period, usually one year. This computation uses "final" goods and services to reach the aggregate production. This means only final goods sold to consumers are included in this calculation. For example, raw materials produced and sold to manufacturers are not included if they are to be used to make final products that are then sold as final goods. GNP reflects only new final products for the measurement period are counted. Markets and transactions in used goods are omitted from GNP. Allocations of GNP are decided by the nation that owns the business unit, not where the goods are sold. For example, funds received from a Volvo manufactured and sold in the United States would be counted as part of Sweden's GNP as they are the owners of the corporation. This means that all proceeds of sales of final goods belong in the national account of the country that claims ownership of the firm that sold the goods.

GDP

Another important measure of economic health is <u>Gross Domestic Product (GDP)</u>. This calculation aggregates all goods and services sold in a specified period but allocates monies determined by where the sale actually takes place, rather than what country owns the business. A Volvo automobile manufactured and sold in the United States would be included in the GNP of America because it was earned in the United States, even though the business owners are Swedish. It follows that to compute GNP from GDP the aggregate total of income from goods sold by other countries must be subtracted from GDP. Gross Domestic Product is a strong indicator of the short-term health of an economy as it measures current aggregate production. It is not as reliable a measure for accounting for the sources, and allocations of a country's income. GDP is a better measure of the state of production in the short term. GNP is better when analyzing sources and uses of income.

Wealth

The definition of wealth is both an objective and subjective one. In normal parlance, wealth is understood to consist primarily of money, land, and investments of an individual. However, wealth includes many subjective factors that cannot be measured by strictly economic values. Additionally, concepts of wealth differ between cultures and societies.
Economic wealth must be measured in relation to all other individuals in the same economic systems. The income of an average middle-class American would make a third world citizen very wealthy. Within the United States, cost-of-living, income, and taxes vary widely. A wealthy person in Iowa may not be considered wealthy is Los Angeles because of differentials in the economic situations of the two places. Additionally, intangibles such as environmental health, health of the individual, quality of life and dozens of other less objective factors all must be accounted for in considering real wealth.

Unemployment

In economics, an unemployed person is one who has the will and capacity to work, but cannot find meaningful employment. The total number of unemployed as a ratio to the entire labor pool is the rate of unemployment. The measurement of people without jobs who are actively seeking work is very difficult. A number of methods for measuring unemployment are used, each with its own flaws and advantages. The comparison of unemployment between different countries is very inaccurate due to different definitions of unemployment and social structures of countries. Unemployment has both significant costs to an economy and society but also provides some economic benefits. Depending on the perspective taken, unemployment at various levels will affect an economy in different ways. More conservative economists argue the marketplace will determine unemployment, while welfare economists call for government action in the field.

There are several types of unemployment recognized by economists. Cyclical unemployment results in recessionary periods of the business cycle when aggregate demand falls. When there is a major change is structure or skill level of an industry, unemployment may result. The advent of computers for word processing made typewriters virtually obsolete, causing those who make, sell, and repair typewriters to be unemployed.
Changes in the market due to shifting demand for certain products affect the employees who produce those goods. If demand for typewriters falls, demand for labor involved with typewriter production and sale also drops. This is also an example of unemployment caused by technological advances. Another type of unemployment is seasonal unemployment where productive activity in

an industry is limited to certain times of the year. Commercial harvesting of oysters is such a seasonal position.

Inflation

Inflation strikes when there is a general price increase of goods and services against one currency. The Consumer Price Index can be used as a measuring tool to compare prices at different times. A fictional "market basket" of commonly consumed staples is measured and charted over a period of time (usually one year). If the price of the representative market basket has gone up, inflation has occurred. For example if a typical basket costs $500 this year as compared to $400 last year for the same basket inflation has risen over a year. Inflation reduces the buying power of money, and if uncontrolled can threaten the entire economy.

An example of runaway inflation occurred in Germany in the 1930's. Inflation was rampant and people literally had to take barrels of money to markets to exchange for goods and services. This rampant inflation helped bring the Nazis to power.

Deflation, the general lowering of prices and the subsequent increase in purchasing power of money is a much less frequent phenomenon.

Recessions

The technical definition of a recession is when a nation's real Gross Domestic Product decreases in two or more consecutive quarters of the fiscal year. Typically, recessions involve falling aggregate demand which causes prices to fall and economic activity to slow. It sometimes occurs when inflation rises quickly, and is combined with a slowing economy. This condition is called "stagflation". In general, recessions are characterized by falling prices. Recessions appear in a more or less regular pattern in capitalistic economies. Recent patterns have indicated a recession may be expected every five to ten years. Most recessions are caused by lack of consumer and business confidence in the future. Some economists encourage government intervention in a recession, while others feel such interference only adds to the problem. The latter group consists of more conservative economists who prefer to let the market determine the level of economic activity.

Depression in the United States

Only once has the United States gone through a massive depression. In the 1920's, massive speculation and investment in stocks caused their prices to rise far above their true value. Adding to the problem was the fact that many of the stocks were purchased on credit, using securities as collateral. When the economy began to contract, share prices fell dramatically and the collateral supporting other stock purchases became worthless. The loans were called, became uncollectible, and triggered a financial panic that led to multiple failures in the banking system. Savings were lost, unemployment soared, and the economy spiraled into a depression. After the election of Franklin Roosevelt in 1932 massive injections of funds were fueled into the economy. Precautions against future bank failures were addressed by federal insurance programs, and speculation in the stock market was regulated as well. Although these measures helped the economy, it was not until the United States entered World War II that it emerged from the effects of the depression.

Commodity markets

Commodities are raw or unfinished components of finished goods yet to be produced. Agricultural products such as soy beans, cotton, and wheat are commodities. Separate markets exist for almost all commodities. Currencies of various countries are also traded as commodities in their own markets. Futures markets exist on many heavily traded commodities, where speculation fuels trading for future delivery of products paid for now. Commodities were one of the first class of goods traded between countries. Modern commodity markets have been safeguarded by a bevy of rules and regulations insuring prompt and accurate payment between countries. International agencies, such as the Bank for International Settlements regulate transaction settlements, insure currencies, set reserve requirements, and generally reduce risks in trade inherent between countries.

Opportunity cost

The opportunity cost of an economic decision is always the cost of what opportunity is sacrificed by making that decision. For example, a person may have enough money for a vacation in Europe, or enough to purchase a new automobile, but not both. The opportunity cost of buying the automobile will be the trip to Europe. These decisions are made usually on the utility of each choice - which would provide the most pleasure to the consumer. In a complex economy, there are many competing factors that provide utility. An individual, firm, or government will always choose what they perceive to be the choice that will be most beneficial given limited resources. These choices are usually not clear-cut and many factors go into some economic decisions. This is more common when companies or governments have to choose between a number of needed and attractive choices. Different parts of society or firms will have much different ideas about the best way in which to utilize their resources.

Price elasticity

When a price is changed, either increased or decreased, there will be a change in the demand for the goods and services. The rate at which demand falls or rises is called the price elasticity of demand. This measurement is usually formulated as a ratio of the changing price and the change in demand. If a price is raised by 20%, and demand falls by 20%, the ratio between them is the price elasticity of demand. Normally, any rise in price will decrease the demand for the goods and services offered. Any decrease in price should raise demand barring other external factors. This theory of price elasticity works best as a model, because in the real economic world there are a huge number of variables that affect price and demand. Usually businesses will test these variables to determine how much a price change will by itself affect demand.

Surplus

A consumer surplus arises when prices fall and buyers realize extra savings which go into a surplus of buying power for purchasers. If for any number of economic factors, suppliers are able to sell at higher prices than they would ordinarily obtain, a supplier surplus exists.
In many areas, particularly commodities and farm products, governments intervene which may cause an artificial surplus. This government intervention usually takes the form of subsidies of some kind, and often represents the government holding a significant surplus itself. Taxes are another area of government intervention that can cause a surplus.
When all the existing surpluses in an economy are aggregated, the sum may be called the total surplus. Welfare economics uses this figure when they consider a new policy, or to examine an existing one.

Income

Income, in common parlance, is the compensation received by economic units during the normal activities of business. This includes monies received from multiple sources including employers, investments, and gifts. In the business world, gross income is the amount a company earns before expenses. Net income is the money the company has earned after paying the costs of doing business. A company's revenue flow starts with monies received from goods and services sold to consumers. From this amount must be subtracted all monies spent in the operations of the business. This includes employees' salaries, costs of production, fixed and variable costs of doing business, and any intangible costs. The resulting figure is the firm's income (or loss). If a profit is made, this may be paid as additional compensation to owners, appropriate tax levies, or reinvested to improve the company's position in some respect. Publicly held corporations may choose to pay their stockholders a dividend.

Per capita income and personal income

The calculation of per capita income is made by taking the total of all monies earned by residents of a particular area divided by the number of inhabitants of the region. Note that per capita income is based on where the individuals live, rather than where they actually physically work. The aggregate of all monies is called Total Personal Income. This figure includes all earnings paid to individuals, transfer payments (social security for example), and investment income from all sources. The relative economic health of a particular area can be measured in part by per capita income and Total Personal Income.

Passive income also is accounted for in Total Personal Income. These are monies derived from rents, private portfolios of stocks and bonds, earned interest from any source, and various payments from pension funds and other employee retirement programs.

Another class of income is derived from government transfer payments. These include various social and disability benefits, as well as compensation for the unemployed.

Perfect competition and monopolistic competition

There is no such thing as perfect competition in the real world. It exists only as an economic model, describing a theoretical market where the base of producers and consumers is so large that they are unable to influence prices. Ideally this would lead to a textbook definition of economic efficiency. For perfect competition to exist, products are essentially the same, each type being an equal substitute for another. Prices are set by the market, and firms must accept this determination. All businesses must have equal access to existing information, raw materials, and the latest technology.

Monopolistic competition has a different set of standards. Usually there are numerous producers and a great number of consumers in any market. No regulations exist to entering or leaving the market, and consumers have more product knowledge and have definite choices between products. These markets give individual companies more influence over their markets. They may raise or lower prices and make adjustments based on the response of the market.

Monopoly and monopsony

When one supplier is the sole seller of a service or product a monopoly is said to exist. There is no competition in a monopolistic economy as there is only one provider or seller and attempts for other firms to enter as competitors are discouraged by economic action of the monopoly holder. This action may be based on better or unique technology, patents on products that allow no competition, and the economic realities of trying to enter a market that is controlled by such a dominating economic entity. These actions and others like them are collectively called blocking the entry to a monopolistic market. These economic actions may or may not be in restraint of trade. Usually in a monopoly there are no ready substitutes for the products being supplied. It can have no true competition forcing consumers to buy from the monopolizing corporation. The company controlling the monopoly can manipulate the price and available supply of the product involved. Artificial shortages can be created that force prices upward. Some monopolies are legal in a sense, a prime example being AT&T before it was broken up by government intervention. Legal monopolies are common in government agencies and institutions, and sometimes exist in specialized private sectors of the economy.

Sometimes an economic phenomenon occurs where there is only a single consumer of a product, and there may be a number of suppliers. This is called monopsony, and only occurs in specialized industries that have large institutional consumers. Cartels differ from monopolies by coordinating the action of a few suppliers to gain economic advantage. Cartels are several firms acting in concert to create an economic advantage. Cartels organize and act as if one business in order to control a finite market.

Oligopoly and oligopsony

When any particular market is controlled by a small group of suppliers an oligopoly is said to exist. In this situation all suppliers are cognizant of each other's activities. When any one firm makes an economic decision, it will impact the activity of all other firms in the oligopoly. There is a great deal of interaction between members of oligopolies, and planning by any one firm must consider the likely responses of all other members. Oligopolies were very common in certain industries but anti-trust laws have limited their power. In the United States, over half of the distinct industries are controlled by oligopolies. These groups are able to stifle competition by buying up resources or by temporarily cutting prices, strategies which are impossible for smaller companies. In this way, oligopolies tend to quash innovation and keep power in the hands of conservative corporations. The power accrued by the members of an oligopoly also gives them the license to make decisions which may be healthy for them but destructive to the society as a whole. The automotive industry's reluctance to pursue economy cars cost millions of American their livelihoods when Japanese manufacturers dominated the 1970s and 80s.

In an oligopsony market there are limited numbers of buyers and an unlimited number of sellers. When a relative few number of businesses are in competition to acquire factors of production this situation is common. Here buyers will have a competitive advantage and will be aware of each other's economic activity. Sometimes a situation arises where there are only a few buyers and a few sellers. This unusual situation results in a bilateral oligopsony.

Taxation

Nations, states, and local governments use taxes to finance their operations and for special purposes. Typical uses of tax revenue are for public utilities, promotion of public safety and defense, reinvesting in capital improvement and replacement projects for the public, general operating expenses of the state, and to fund public and welfare services. Other uses for tax revenues include social benefits for retired and disabled citizens, public transportation systems, compensation for those unable to work, educational uses, public health and healthcare systems, and waste removal operations. Governments also use taxes to stimulate or contract the economy, alter resource allocations in the economic system, insure an equitable tax burden on all citizens, and to change patterns of income distribution for members of a society. Taxation and its revenues have become an important proactive tool for economists attempting to fine tune macroeconomic activities.

International trade and tariffs

Tariffs are in effect, a tax on goods imported from other countries. Goods cannot be delivered and sold before a tariff is paid. Tariffs have broad implications in international trade and consequently in relations between nations. Tariffs may be calculated by the weight of goods, or as a percentage of the value of the item. The latter case is termed an ad valorem tax. Sometimes governments impose tariffs as a purely money making function, and these are termed revenue tariffs. Tariffs are widely used by countries to protect their own exports and to defend their own industries from competition from abroad. Tariffs add to the price of imported goods, affording a price advantage to local products. A protective tariff can be so high as to be prohibitive, so that no imports are economically viable. Tariffs have become both political and economic weapons for competing nations. Tariffs have historically been opposed by "free traders", who believe unfettered trade is the healthiest economic environment and works to the benefit of all countries involved.

Trade between nations

Commerce between nations, the trading of products and service functions from one country to another, is called international trade. Trade between countries was very limited in the premodern era. As the capabilities for shipping and transport increased, so did the opportunities for international commerce. Today it constitutes a significant portion of many countries economies. The rise of companies doing business in many countries has contributed to the increase of international trade. The term "globalization", has come to mean the spreading network of connecting economic ties throughout the world. International trade is used as a political as well as economic strategy in relations between nations. As countries seek new markets in order to grow and prosper, international commerce is an ideal avenue for economic growth. Tariff policy is another weapon used in geo-politics as nations strive to prosper in an increasingly competitive world. Economic success for many individual firms depends on their ability to develop international markets for their goods and services.

Balance of trade

The term balance of trade refers to the relationship between the values of imported goods and services and exported goods and services. Every country hopes to have a positive balance of trade. This means they have sold more goods and services abroad than they have purchased. Such a positive balance of trade, (called a surplus), indicates a strong economy with good international markets. Conversely, a negative balance of trade, (called a deficit), can indicate some fundamental weakness in a country's ability to profitably engage in international commerce. The exchange of raw materials, manufactured goods, agricultural goods, transportation, and travel are all considered in determination of a country's balance of trade.
Trade restrictions, including tariffs and other regulations can weaken a country's trading position. Widely fluctuating exchange rates may cast uncertainty on the wisdom of trading with a particular country. Social and political environments have a direct effect on international commerce. Basic economic indicators such as inflation, price levels, and aggregate demand and supply all have a bearing on the balance of payments. Ultimately, it is the totality of all these issues that may determine the success of a country in international business.

Free trade and trade barriers

The exchange of goods and services across international boundaries can be termed "free trade" only if the traded products are untaxed and no restrictions apply. Trade barriers of one kind or another or tariffs make free trade impossible and are a deterrent to commerce between nations. Trade barriers may include taxes on imports, known as tariffs, limited amounts of a specific product that may be exported to a country, and other laws, restrictions, taxes or regulations limiting the unfettered commerce between countries.

Free trade is also promoted by economic policies that foster the movement of both labor and capital between countries. This climate of economic cooperation is needed to insure a working economic relationship between trading partners. Regional trade agreements or treaties often outline the rules and regulations of commerce between nations. A country cedes some of its economic independence when engaging in free trade. There are both costs and benefits that must be assessed.

Trade pacts

A trade pact is a broad agreement between two or more nations that specifies which forms of production and consumption are ideal and which are undesirable. This type of agreement attempts to increase productive efficiency through the facilitation of free trade (the international exchange of goods and services without tariffs or trade barriers, such as import quotas). Trade pacts often come under political scrutiny for their roles in increasing economic interdependence between entities or altering traditional economic customs. There are several different types of trade pacts.

Profit

The word profit is derived from the Latin and means 'to go forward or advance". In an economic sense, profit is the gain made from an economic transaction made by a business or individual. Profit may be defined in a multitude of ways, depending on the economic system and the method of accounting within that system. In investment transactions, profit is understood to be the return over time of an input of land, labor, and capital. In business concerns this is usually expressed as a rate of return for the assets utilized. Most business concerns measure profit as the difference between revenue received and costs. Economists broaden this definition to include the return from an economic action when the opportunity costs of all other possible choices are considered. The drive for businesses to maximize profits is considered a stimulus to economic activity. It provides motivation and actual rewards for astute economic decisions.

Cost-benefit analysis

The determination of the best possible economic action in a situation is often formally or intuitively a result of a cost-benefit computation. An individual must ask what the total costs will be in any decision in relation to the total benefits which may be reasonably predicted. Analyzing several alternatives using this approach will yield the best decision given the information available. In business decisions this usually means what amount of resources must be used to gain a specified return or profit. Such cost-benefit calculations are not limited to money. Subjective factors must be considered and sometimes an arbitrary monetary value placed on them. Economic decisions, particularly on the part of governments, must weigh economic, quality of life, political, and social elements into this analysis. For example, a government decision to drill for oil in a natural habitat will include economic considerations, as well as the impact of the decision on the well being of the society as a whole. Since almost all economic actions occur over time, the future costs and profits must be considered from a present-value perspective.